Serving God in Today's
CITIES
Facing the Challenge of
URBANIZATION

Patrick Johnstone with Dean Merrill

gmi

Serving God in Today's Cities: Facing the Challenge of Urbanization
By Patrick Johnstone with Dean Merrill
Foreword by Dr. Ed Stetzer

Published by GMI
PO Box 63719
Colorado Springs, CO 80962

ISBN 978-1-941405-12-3 (Print edition)
ISBN 978-1-941405-13-0 (e-book edition)

Why We Publish

GMI is passionate about helping Kingdom workers make Spirit-led decisions that advance the global Church.

Our Mission

GMI leverages research and technology to create, cultivate, and communicate mission information leading to insight that inspires Kingdom service.

Accessible Resources

GMI is committed to creating missions research resources that are accessible, engaging and actionable. If you have ideas about how we can apply, contextualize and translate our research to help Kingdom workers worldwide, contact the Publisher at: publisher@gmi.org.

Publisher and CEO: Jon Hirst
Publishing Coordinator: Barb Beyer
Editorial Consultant: Steve Rabey
Design: Allison Jones, Julie Evans
Proofing: Susan G Mathis

Explore other resources at www.gmi.org/GMIBooks

Publisher's Foreword

We make many decisions every day. Not every choice has eternal consequences (Paper or plastic? Decaf or regular?). But many do.

Jon Hirst

When decisions involve your faith walk, your calling and your ministry, the decisions you make can be life changing. Facing such important decisions can seem daunting.

We hope this resource helps guide your decision making. That's because at GMI, our passion is helping Kingdom workers like you make Spirit-led decisions that advance the global Church.

We're honored to bring you the best available data combined with compelling stories and narrative that give you a unique perspective as you seek God's wisdom.

We hope and pray this resource will help you discern God's guidance for your life. If this resource does help you, could you please let me know?

Write us at publisher@gmi.org and share your decision story with us so that we can celebrate with you as God uses you to advance His Kingdom.

God bless you in your service!

In Him,
Jon Hirst
Publisher/President, GMI

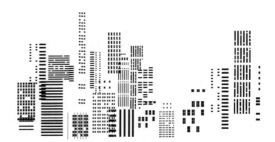

Foreword

In my work at LifeWay Research and through my blog, I regularly attempt to call the Church's attention to cultural trends that affect the ways in which we share the gospel and accomplish the Great Commission in our local churches and our personal walks with Christ. I am a missiologist so, well, that's what we are supposed to help people do.

Ed Stetzer, Ph.D.

Whether I'm pointing people to the usefulness of social media or explaining the importance of welcoming other cultures and backgrounds, I serve the Church by helping it better understand and interact with the world around it. One of the most recent trends missiologists have been keeping an eye on is the urbanization of the world and how such migration affects the ways in which we plant churches and do mission.

"The city" is an emerging phrase that seems to be embraced by a growing number of Christians. I intentionally say they are embracing the phrase, because I do not think that all are actually embracing the city. Rather most are simply embracing the idea of embracing the city.

Whatever it is that we say about the city, the truth is the church is often absent from the urban context. Tim Keller, founding pastor of Redeemer Presbyterian Church in New York City and one who is at the forefront of this renewed call to reach the cities, says that people are moving into the cities faster than the church is.

Part of the reason is that urban ministry is complex ministry. A diversity of cultures, races, and socioeconomic statuses make for a beautiful mosaic of the people of God, but working among the diversity of Miami can be more complicated than ministering among a more homogenous group in rural Nebraska.

When cultural differences collide, things can get messy. But the beauty of the gospel is how it brings unity in the midst of what often seems to be chaos.

As Paul is writing to the first century churches, most often located in important cities of the day, he constantly brings them back to the unity that belongs to them in Christ—despite all the differences they may see and experience when the church gathers as a body.

He reminds the Corinthian church that they have all been baptized into one body through one Spirit (1 Corinthians 12:12). He tells the Galatians that the distinctions so often made in their society—Jew or Greek, slave or free, male or female—were unimportant considering the oneness they had in Christ (Galatians 3:28).

Paul spent time in these cities and wrote letters to the churches there, not because he felt like rural people didn't matter, but because he recognized the influence that radiates from the urban centers. It's why he spent over two years in Ephesus. He was reaching the city, which in turn was reaching the whole province of Asia (Acts 19:10).

So urban ministry is important, and the growing passion for it is encouraging, but if we're going to properly minister to people in urban areas, we have to better understand modern urbanization and the complexities that make up urban ministry.

I think "God of this City" by Bluetree (popularized by Chris Tomlin) is a great, powerful song that gets at the longing in the hearts of those wanting to do urban ministry—Christians want to embrace, engage, serve, and reach cities. Fair enough. It is a good thing, and something we should be passionate about.

As one who grew up on Long Island outside of New York City and planted my first church in Buffalo, New York among the urban poor, I love the concept of "urban ministry."

Yet, I am convinced that you cannot love a city if you do not know a city.

Now, full disclosure, I am biased. I run a research firm and we do city research, so you should be aware of that. I run a research firm because I believe that we need to know so we can engage. If you don't properly understand the context in which you want to minister until after you start ministering there, your ministry will likely be more frustrating than fruitful.

That's where books like *Serving God in Today's Cities* come in. This book from Patrick Johnstone and Dean Merrill serves the church by helping its leaders better understand the cities in which they're planting churches, living on mission, and sharing the gospel.

The fact is, the how of ministry is, in many ways, shaped by the who, when, and where of culture. So, in order to reach the city, we have to come with a missionary mindset. We have to love the city, and know the city, to engage the city.

Serving God in Today's Cities can help the church in their effort to develop a missional attitude toward urban areas. But we need to do it now because cities are growing faster than most of us even realize. Patrick Johnstone and Dean Merrill report that by the end of the century, the world will be over 90 percent urban. That is an astonishing statistic. But perhaps more surprisingly, he says we're already halfway there.

As we go to the cities—not just the idea, but the reality, tools help us to engage them more effectively. I'm thankful for the hard work and in-depth research they put into this book, and my hope is that it will be a useful tool for urban ministers of the gospel for years to come, even as we approach 90 percent urbanization of the world.

Ed Stetzer, Ph.D.
www.edstetzer.com

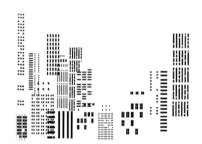

CONTENTS

Publisher's Foreword iii

Foreword iv

Introduction viii

Part 1: Eyes To See 1

   1 The First Urban Century 3

   2 Cities: Headache or Opportunity? 17

   3 What God Thinks of Cities 21

Part 2: Eight Critical Responses 29

   4 Action 1: Pray Together 31

   5 Action 2: Exegete the City 41

   6 Action 3: Push Against Urban Poverty 49

   7 Action 4: Reach Out to Diasporas 57

   8 Action 5: Form Healthy Churches 65

   9 Action 6: Confront Sinful Structures 75

   10 Action 7: Address Real Human Pain Directly 81

   11 Action 8: Embrace a Wider Vision 89

12 Conclusion: Greater Things are Still to Come 95

Notes 98

Featured Ministries 100

Going Deeper: Resources From GMI 103

Introduction

I (throughout this book, "I" refers to me) have served as an active missionary for 52 years, first as an urban evangelist, and then an international mobilizer of prayer and workers for the least evangelized on earth. The Great Commission of Matthew 28:16-20, with Jesus' core injunction to disciple all nations, has been fundamental to my ministry. My work in producing the various editions of *Operation World* was a big part of that.

My latter book, *The Future of the Global Church*, was specifically written in 2011 as a handover of my public ministry to a new generation of mobilizers by giving a global vision and the tools to portray it. This book covered much ground in its 240 pages, but these could give only some broad strokes of the challenges and possibilities for future ministry.

Jon Hirst, the CEO of GMI, had the vision of expanding on some of that book's themes by publishing a series of more specific books, of which this volume on urbanization is the first.

Dean Merrill was approached to do the main task of compiling the text, drawing upon hours of interaction with me and with further research. I have been delighted to work closely with Dean in the writing of this book and am very pleased with the results as well as the efficiency with which he has accomplished it.

My prayer is that God will use this effort both to call new workers to the world's cities and to refine existing ministries.

Patrick Johnstone
WEC International
Author Emeritus, *Operation World*

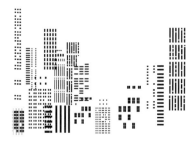

PART ONE:
EYES TO SEE

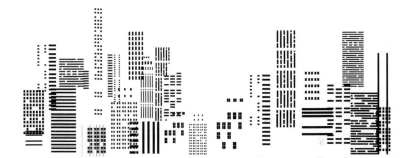

CHAPTER 1
The First Urban Century

Congested. Creative. Loud. Artistic. Sinful. Busy. High crime. High earnings. Easy anonymity. Easy networking. Hyperactive. Hip. Boisterous. Innovative. Ruthless. Soaring. Intimidating. Invigorating.

The world's cities are all of the above, and more. You can love the energy of Hong Kong or Rome or Los Angeles, or you can despise their hectic (and expensive) lifestyles. The minute you start to think about ministry in an urban center, a rush of possibilities floods your mind, only to collide a few seconds later with an undertow of complications.

A recent study in India—one of the world's fastest-growing, fastest-changing societies—asked city dwellers about "the pace of modern life." Forty-nine percent liked it (more young people than older, understandably), while 37 percent disliked it, and 13 percent couldn't make up their minds. Those with a college degree and those with high incomes—in other words, the "haves"—were more positive than the less educated and poor. Yet in the same survey, 52 percent (and 62 percent of those with a college degree) said, "Our traditional way of life is getting lost." More than eight out of ten Indians bemoaned the fact that the rich were getting richer while the poor were getting poorer.[1]

All around the world, and especially on the continents of Asia and Africa, urban growth is an unstoppable train. As Ray Bakke, a leading U.S. advocate for city ministry, says to his audiences, "You have an urban future, whether you like it or not."

What the Numbers Tell Us

The most recent United Nations numbers say that the global population—currently at 7.2 billion souls—will add another 53 percent by the end of this century, reaching somewhere around 11 billion.[2] More to our point, *90 percent* of those 11 billion will live in cities.

It is hard to remember that only as recently as the year 1800, the urban figure was a mere 3 percent; the other 97 percent lived in rural areas. Now the tables have been completely turned. Thus the 21st century will be the first urban century in human history.

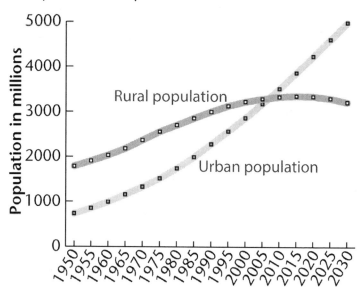

The tipping point, statisticians now believe, came around 2007 or 2008, when the world's urban population outpaced the rural population. Since that point, the urban line only keeps climbing, while the rural line gradually declines.

Some may wonder what defines the word *urban*. How big a city does it signify? The U.N. Population Division has set no global metric; it simply collects and reports what the 230-some individual countries consider to be "urban." In some nations, 50,000 people in a given area is the threshold; in others, lesser figures are used. Regardless, the reality is that more and more people on this planet are carrying on their daily lives in the close quarters we all understand to be urban.

And in some individual cities, the swelling size is taking on startling proportions. Pause for a minute to study these Top Ten lists:

Top 10 Cities in 2000		Top 10 Cities in 2025		Top 10 Cities in 2050	
City, Country	mil	City, Country	mil	City, Country	mil
Tokyo, Japan	28	Mumbai, India	30	Lagos, Nigeria	64
Mexico City	18	Lagos, Nigeria	30	Mumbai, India	50
Mumbai, India	18	Tokyo, Japan	29	Karachi, Pakistan	50
São Paulo, Brazil	17	Karachi, Pakistan	25	Dhaka, Bangladesh	49
New York, USA	17	Dhaka, Bangladesh	24	Kolkata, India	34
Shanghai, China	14	Kolkata, India	21	Kinshasa, Congo-DR	34
Lagos, Nigeria	13	Mexico City	21	Delhi, India	33
Los Angeles, USA	13	São Paulo, Brazil	21	Shanghai, China	30
Kolkata, India	13	Shanghai, China	21	Addis Ababa, Eth	30
Buenos Aires, Arg	12	Delhi, India	20	Tokyo, Japan	30

The world's 10 most populous cities

Think about those numbers. How big and overwhelming would one city be with 50 million residents (for example, Mumbai or Karachi in 2050)? *Answer:* Imagine today's New York City metroplex *times three*. It boggles the mind. And Lagos, Nigeria, is slated to be even larger by mid-century.

Now notice that by then, all of the top ten will be in Africa (3) and Asia (7). Furthermore, only two of the ten (Shanghai and Tokyo) are set to have a highly developed infrastructure—adequate roads, water systems, electrical supply, mass transit, governmental services; most of the others will be struggling to meet the basic needs of their rapidly growing populations.

Meanwhile, all five of the Western Hemisphere cities on the 2000 list (Mexico City, Sao Paulo, New York, Los Angeles, Buenos Aires) will have dropped off by 2050, while Tokyo will have slid from first place to tenth. Only one city in Europe will have as many as 10 million residents—and that will be Istanbul (which lies only partly on European soil; the rest is across the Bosphorus strait in Asia).

To visualize the massive change, compare the following two maps:

The World's Megacities in 2000

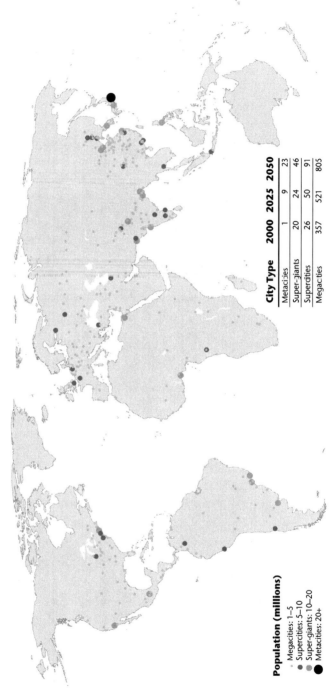

City Type	2000	2025	2050
Metacities	1	9	23
Super-giants	20	24	46
Supercities	26	50	91
Megacities	357	521	805

Population (millions)

- Megacities: 1–5
- Supercities: 5–10
- Super-giants: 10–20
- Metacities: 20+

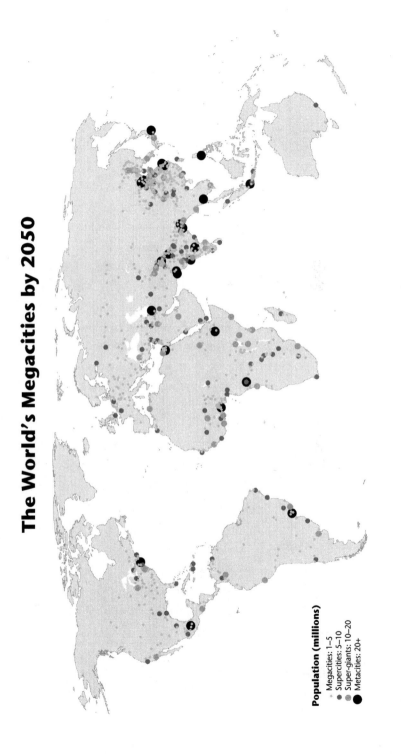

The World's Megacities by 2050

Population (millions)
- Megacities: 1–5
- Supercities: 5–10
- Super-giants: 10–20
- Metacities: 20+

Who are all These People?

The urban increases of the 21st century will come from two sources:

1. New children born to those already living in cities, as birth rates in large parts of the world keep running higher than death rates (for a variety of reasons, not the least of which is better medical care for expectant mothers and the babies they bear). Fewer maternal and newborn deaths is a good thing, of course.

2. Inflow from those moving into the city in search of (a) jobs, (b) more education for themselves or their children, or (c) safety from war or harassment in their home area—whether that be 50 kilometers away or 5,000.

As a result, most cities are becoming noticeably more cross-cultural. Vancouver on the west coast of Canada now has more Sikhs than anywhere outside the Punjab region of northern India. Their colorful turbans can be seen all throughout the city. San Francisco is 38 percent Asian. London is now only 60 percent "white English"; the rest of Londoners are Asian, black, and of mixed heritage. Brussels, the capital of the European Union, has only 32 percent indigenous Flemish and Walloon French inhabitants; the rest are of foreign origin from across Europe and other continents. A quarter of the city's population is Muslim.

Tim Svoboda, international urban missions director for Youth with a Mission (YWAM), writes, "In the past, missions was primarily about going over the ocean, through the jungle, across the desert to reach the remote. Today, missions is about crossing the street in the cities where we live."[3]

No Guarantees

As you might expect, many of the urban newcomers are young adults. They may enroll in a college; they may find employment as factory workers, laborers on construction sites, nurses or other aides in the health care field, clerks in shops, street sellers, or some other job.

Along the way, they may meet someone they wish to marry. If they are able to establish themselves, their parents or other relatives back home—siblings, cousins, etc.—may follow their trail to the city and attempt to duplicate their success.

But if they cannot gain a foothold in the urban economy, dark consequences await. Desperate young women may be lured (or forced) into the sex trade. Desperate young men may resort to theft and violence in order to get food. Drugs come into play as a way to numb anxiety. For some, the selling of drugs appears to be the only way to get money. Affordable housing is often hard to find, and the new arrivals may wind up wishing they had never ventured toward the bright lights. But going home again is hardly an option.

All of these social and economic dynamics come into play as we look at the prospects for urban ministry.

First Glimpses

My early interest in the urbanized world came not because I was intrigued with cities per se, but rather because of my concern for one country: South Africa. I was moved by such books as Alan Paton's *Cry, the Beloved Country* and Trevor Huddleston's *Naught for Your Comfort*. They vividly described the grimness of the apartheid system, especially in the black urban townships that had sprung up with South Africa's industrialization during World War II.

Such cities were an alien world to me, of course. My family was relatively well off—my father a doctor in a rural area of Gloucestershire in England. My heart was set on being a research scientist, and so I enrolled at the University of Bristol.

There, everything changed. I became a Christian during my first year of studying chemistry and was well discipled by a godly theological student. He brought me to meet other Christian students of the UCCF (Universities and Colleges Christian Fellowship). One midweek evening, Glyndwr Davies of the Dorothea Mission, a South African agency, spoke passionately to our group about its evangelistic and discipling ministry. The slides he showed vividly portrayed the harsh realities and spiritual need (but without the smells!). Immediately I knew deep in my heart that God was in this and was calling me to serve with that agency in Africa.

I completed my degree but turned down offers to go on for a Ph.D. I left for Africa in 1962 as a young man of 24.

Since the colonial powers were granting independence to many countries, this was an extraordinary time of change all across the African continent. Decades of turmoil and wars would soon follow, along with massive urbanization and the explosive rise of indigenous Christianity. In many ways, the Dorothea Mission was a pioneer in the cities; almost all other mission activity was directed to rural and tribal areas.

My introduction to the black townships was dramatic and sudden. I was welcomed at the Johannesburg airport by the mission founder and director, Hans von Staden, a great man for vision and prayer. After shaking my hand and loading my baggage into his car, he said, "I am going to show you something."

> I stared out the window at the densely packed array of shacks made from scrap metal, discarded wood, corrugated iron, asbestos sheeting, and pieces of cardboard, all held together with nails, string, and wire. More than 20,000 people lived here in great squalor on a square mile of land.

What he had in mind was not Joburg's towering office buildings or the well-manicured lawns of the jacaranda-lined suburbs. Instead, we drove directly to a black shantytown near the white township of Edenvale. This grim settlement had sprung up a few years earlier to house the black workers who were flooding into the cities seeking a better life. I stared out the window at the densely packed array of shacks made from scrap metal, discarded wood, corrugated iron, asbestos sheeting, and pieces of cardboard, all held together with nails, string, and wire. More than 20,000 people lived here in great squalor on a square mile of land. This time I could not miss the accompanying smell, or the deep sense of hopelessness and pain for these city people amid the mud and the open sewers.

Hans von Staden then shared his heart. "This is what moved me to start the mission back in 1943. Nothing was being done to meet the spiritual needs of these people."

I was overwhelmed. He went on to explain, "The physical needs are so great, but the spiritual needs are the greatest of all. Once these dear people become believers in Christ, their lives are transformed, and the money they have is not used for beer or drugs, but for food and improving their housing and the education of their children."

As we drove away, I felt a mix of burden and panic. *How can I possibly make a difference? Is this what my working conditions will be for the years ahead?*

I plunged into completing my Bible training at the mission Bible college in Pretoria. Due to apartheid's rules, our African workers had to be trained at another institution on the other side of the city. But we would meet up on weekends for ministry in townships with open-air meetings, house visitation, and tract distribution. Night after night, we saw the message of hope and change break through lives ravaged by violence, drunkenness, and in some cases, the occult.

Soon after my training was completed, I was asked to be the leader of a team. This forced me to come face-to-face with the cruel bureaucracy of the apartheid system. In every township where we sought to erect our evangelistic tent, my African co-workers had to obtain a stamp in their passbooks to permit them to stay there. The officials who granted this were petty white officials who were often deliberately difficult and even rude. In such cases, I went along with my co-workers to ensure they were not unjustly denied.

Our pattern of ministry in the townships was to preach the gospel in every possible way, with the goal of making young disciples who would be strong enough to stand on their own feet once we left, and where possible, be linked to a good congregation of believers among the many churches now springing up in these urban slums. We would pray in the mornings, house-visit and hold open-air meetings in the afternoons, then conduct nightly evangelistic meetings in the tent. We all participated in the preaching, and most of us became at least quadrilingual (using up to four languages) in the process, and some of my African co-workers could speak six languages!

What was the fruit? Hundreds of thousands had good exposure to the gospel, and thousands came to the point of decision for Christ. Others struggled to let go of the fear of people or their involvement with witchcraft. But many of these seekers went on to become true disciples and some went into full-time ministry for the Lord.

One such was Stephen Lungu. He was converted in Salisbury (now Harare) in Rhodesia (now Zimbabwe) in 1962 during a dramatic Dorothea evangelistic campaign held in the midst of severe unrest against the white minority government of the time. As a small child, Steve's parents had had a huge row, and both walked out on the other, effectually abandoning their four children. They had no contact with their children for years, thinking that the other would be caring for them. Steve's one ambition, as a teenager, was to find and kill his mother. As an angry young man, he became involved in crime and was also in a gang.

One night he carried a petrol bomb as he went with his gang to disrupt the tent meeting. But as he sat looking around, the South African preacher, Shadrach Maloka, told how Christ had found him as an abandoned orphan who had become a *tsosti* (teenage gangster). Steve was riveted. Toward the end of the meeting he went forward, still carrying the petrol bomb with him, and asked Shadrach, "Can your Jesus help me?"

Shadrach led him to Jesus that night, and Steve's life was changed forever. He went to Bible school and joined the mission in which he served as a worker for the next 18 years. I was his first team leader, and he became my main "Timothy" as I sought to prepare all my workers for future leadership.

In fact, he took over the leadership from me in 1977. He was later asked by Michael Cassidy to join African Enterprise, an African evangelistic mission, and eventually he became their global ambassador and CEO—a mighty man of God. His autobiography, *Out of the Black Shadows,* is still in print today. One of the joys of his faith-filled life was that he was used by God not only to forgive his parents, but also lead them to Jesus.

Back at the beginning, during my Bible school days, I had met another U.K. worker named Jill Amsden. In time, we wished to marry. But the mission required that, in light of the tough working conditions and much travel, all workers should remain single for six years. So we faced a long wait.

Finally, we were wed during our first home leave, and when we returned to Africa, we began our service together evangelizing in the cities and towns of Rhodesia. Those were years of national turmoil, which culminated in the end of white rule in 1979-80. Yet it was also a time of spiritual harvest.

Increasingly my African co-workers took on more and more leadership of the work, so that I was able to give time to compiling the first two editions of *Operation World* (published in 1972 and 1978). This was a miracle, seeing that we had no suitable libraries, and the postal services with over half the world were cut, due to sanctions imposed on the government of Prime Minister Ian Smith.

Little has Changed

These are not just tales of a long-ago past. The urban poor are with us to this very day and will be on into the future. The terminology may vary by location, from "slums" (India) to "townships" (Africa) to "favelas" (Brazil), but the daily reality is much the same. Later in this book (chapters 6, 9, and 10), we will examine the best practices for infusing Christian hope and light into these desperate pools of humanity.

> Whether they live in "slums," "townships," or "favelas," the daily reality of the urban poor is much the same.

My wife and I thought we had seen the worst conditions in southern Africa—until we and our three small children spent a year on the Operation Mobilization ship *MV Logos* traveling from port to port in gospel outreach. Our first stop was Mumbai. I was horrified to see poverty at a depth I had not encountered up to then. Babies had been left on the pavement under a cloth while their parents scavenged for food, or for paper and metal to resell. I had to step over the infant as I walked along the street!

On we went to Calcutta (now Kolkata). In one slum area, I saw that it had grown up on the bank of a drainage canal. I knew that this entire city was prone to periodic flooding of the Hooghly River that bisects it; the elevation is less than 10 meters above sea level. So I asked my guide, "What will happen to all these people when the next flood comes?"

"A lot of them will die," he answered matter-of-factly. He took it for granted. The West Bengal state, of which Kolkata is the capital, was ruled then (and for decades thereafter) by the Communist Party, and we saw its red flag with a white hammer-and-sickle everywhere. But we dared to hold an open-air evangelistic meeting in front of party headquarters, and it wasn't long before stones began flying at us.

But even amid the hostility, we began to notice that the caste system, which has bound Indian society for centuries, was gradually starting to erode in the urban setting. Unlike in the villages, where everyone knew their place and would not dare to step out of it, city life had a way of encouraging change. The poor could at least think about attempting something outside the boundaries of their preordained status.

Since that time, India has seen a steady rise in aspirations among the Dalits (traditionally, the "untouchables" or lowest caste). They are beginning to find their voice and even sway elections. Urban living has clearly been a factor in this shift.

A New Missions Epoch

But of course, cities are more than an amalgam of the poor and desperate. They are also home to the upwardly mobile, the rising middle class in many nations, as well as the power elite. When our ship docked at Singapore, we found quite the opposite of Mumbai. The city was nearly spotless, to the point that even chewing gum was banned. At that moment, there was a discussion about whether to plant fruit trees in the median strips of the various highways for beautification. Wouldn't people try to dash across the busy lanes of traffic to steal the fruit? No, the answer came; the government would tell everyone not to do that—and they would obey!

Here we found the ethnic Chinese majority responding rapidly to the gospel—despite living alongside a large Muslim Malay minority, and Muslim and Buddhist majorities in the surrounding nations. Churches were growing fast; it was God's time for that city-state.

We were told that 10 percent of primary school children were Christian, 20 percent of those in secondary school, 30 percent in tertiary education, and 40 percent of all medical students. Thus, the more educated a Singaporean was, the more likely he or she was to be Christian. We eagerly joined in to support and strengthen these believers.

To this day, the growth continues. Singapore has become a strong missionary-sending country and a center for Christian leadership and ministries, not only across Asia but also beyond. It is a great example of how a key city can impact the entire world.

Onward we sailed to the ports of Australia, New Zealand, and the South Pacific. Each place brought us new insights. By the time the year was finished, Jill and I were fully aware that a new epoch was dawning. Missionary effort in the 19th and early 20th centuries had been largely rural. The famous David Livingstone, to cite just one example, had pushed into the dark heart of Africa bearing the good news. The needs of the rural world were so great. And of course, we honored the legacy of those early pioneers for the gospel.

But now, we realized that the mission mindset must change. Without neglecting those in the "uttermost parts," we must embrace the call to the world's swarming cities.

I went to visit the teams of WEC International (the mission we joined at the end of our year aboard the *Logos*) up in three northern provinces of Thailand, near Chiang Mai. They were earnestly working to bring Christ to the rural people there. But one day I asked the field leader, "During the course of a year, how many converts do you lose to the cities, such as Bangkok?"

"Oh, a lot," he answered.

"So when are we going to plant churches in Bangkok?" I persisted.

"No," he replied, "this is where we need to be"—even though there was a steady hemorrhage of the most effective Christians toward the urban areas.

I am glad to report that later on, further discussions and prayer led the WEC team to release workers to move to Bangkok for church planting ministry.

How Then Shall We Minister?

Such adjustments are vital for all Kingdom work, by all agencies, if we are to be effective in the world's first urban century. We cannot keep doing things the way we've always done them. We must say to ourselves and to each other, "In light of urbanization—which is only going to keep growing—how then shall we minister?"

In the next two chapters, we shall look at:

- How we think about cities—our assumptions, prejudices, and attitudes
- How *God* thinks about cities, as evidenced throughout his Word, in both Old and New Testaments.

Following that, we will delve into eight specific strategies for advancing the gospel in any urban setting, regardless of location. Current examples will be given for each of the strategies, to establish that they are more than just theoretical.

There is an old proverb that says, "Time and tide wait for no man." The tide of change that is now surging toward the world's cities is not going to stop. We who serve the King of kings must accept it, understand it, and take action.

CHAPTER 2

Cities: Headache or Opportunity?

Sports coaches all over the world know that games are won or lost on much more than just physical talent. Whether playing cricket in India, *fútbol* in Argentina, or hockey in Sweden, mental attitude is a huge factor. The team that *thinks* it can win is far more likely to come out on top.

The opponent may be ranked higher, its players paid better, their equipment and technology more advanced. But what goes on inside the mind determines as much as any of these factors. And when the underdog team prevails, fans are ecstatic, sportswriters wax eloquent, and even movie producers pay attention (as witnessed by such films as *Miracle* or *Glory Road*).

Here at the beginning of this book on urban ministry, let us ask ourselves: What do we *think* about the world's cities?

Reasons to be Pessimistic

Ministry in an urban environment can be daunting for any number of causes:

- Urban dwellers seem busier, more preoccupied, less willing to engage in conversation with a stranger.
- City life is expensive. Everything from taxes to restaurants to property (for homes or church buildings) costs more.

- Cities are generally more dangerous; by contrast, fewer people in rural areas feel the need to lock up their homes or belongings so extensively.
- Organized crime (extortion, prostitution, and drug trafficking, among others) is almost always city-based.
- Political corruption seems to develop more extensively in urban environments.
- Traffic congestion is a daily frustration.
- Long-standing traditions of morality are more easily abandoned once people fade into a cityscape. Old customs and taboos break down.
- Sociologists report that the closer people live together, the less interest they take in getting to know one another's lives—or in responding to one another's misfortunes. Neighbors can be living within a few steps of tragedy, and remain apathetic.
- Air pollution is definitely more serious in the cities. Among the worst: Delhi, India; Karachi, Pakistan; Dakar, Senegal; Dhaka, Bangladesh; Beijing, China. Foul air kills seven million people each year, says the World Health Organization—more than malaria and AIDS combined.[4]
- Missionaries are less special or noticed in big cities; after all, there are NGOs of all kinds and stripes (religious and secular) on nearly every avenue. Some of them have far bigger budgets than the missionary. It's easy to get lost in the crowd of would-be helpers.

"If we reach the cities, we will reach
the nation. If we fail in the cities,
they will become a cesspool that infects
the entire nation."

- Dwight L. Moody

Reasons to be Optimistic

On the other hand, those whom God has called to advance His Kingdom in the great cities of the world have cause to be positive in their outlook. Some of these advantages are purely physical and economic, while others are cultural and personal. Consider these factors:

- Social mobility is greater. One's skill counts for more than one's background. A person is not locked into a certain trade, for example. (In fact, I predict that the caste system of India will steadily founder upon the rocks of that nation's urbanization.)
- The act of moving to a city is an upheaval, which opens up the person for various kinds of change. Personal conversion is a much greater possibility. If parents or other family members disapprove, the new Christian can move along to alternative social networks. Decisions in the city are not nearly as collective as they are in village life.
- Newcomers arrive in the city with a great thirst for relationships. They say to themselves, "In this great mass of humanity, where can I find someone who would learn my name and be my friend?" This is a great opportunity for the church to welcome them.
- Physical distances for the Christian worker in a city are definitely shorter (despite the traffic). You don't need a mission plane to fly from village to village.
- Communication infrastructures are more developed and reliable. (Wireless internet actually works, and at faster speeds.) Services for printing and audiovisual production are nearby.
- Mass media (television, radio, newspapers, magazines) are at hand. Bookstores abound.
- Nonstop international flights are plentiful.
- Medical care, including specialties, is nearby if needed.
- Metropolitan people tend to be more literate, more highly educated. As such, they wield a greater influence on the society. The "movers and shakers" tend to headquarter in cities. If won to Jesus, they can make a real difference in their whole country.
- The same is true for immigrants to the city. If they come to know Christ, they can leverage their familiarity in language-specific communities back home, even if such societies are deemed "closed" to outsiders.
- Many large cities operate in just one language. Unlike in a jungle setting, Kingdom workers do not have to learn a new language every time they change locales. This greatly simplifies ministry efforts and initiatives.[5]

Even the new arrivals coming into a city from elsewhere know they must quickly grasp the prevailing language in order to understand the culture, get a job, or handle daily tasks. The tribal person who, at great personal risk, strikes out from the Sumatran rainforest to seek their future in Jakarta knows they will have to employ the Indonesian language right away.

- For the expatriate missionary and family, daily living can be more accommodating. There are almost always international schools for the children, an international church, a fellowship of other missionaries, and readily available diplomatic services (consulates).

- Most important of all: Here within one metropolis are vast numbers, even millions, of people for whom Christ died.

A Mandate to Heed

In light of these realities, Kingdom people have no basis on which to avoid the cities of the 21st century. Whatever apprehensions or past prejudices we may carry must be laid aside. We cannot afford to let our traditions get in the way of the waiting harvest across the world's metroplexes.

Dwight L. Moody, the late-19th-century evangelist, grew up in a rural village of fewer than 2,000 souls along a peaceful river in northwestern Massachusetts, USA. God's future for him, however, lay in the bustling, industrial "City of the Big Shoulders," Chicago, Illinois. There he started Sunday schools, then began preaching, and eventually founded a Bible institute and a publishing house, both of which survive and thrive to this day within a mile of downtown. His personal impact over more than three decades was felt all across not only his own country but the British Isles as well. Moody said, with his characteristic bluntness:

"If we reach the cities, we will reach the nation. If we fail in the cities, they will become a cesspool that infects the entire nation."

Now more than a century after Moody's death, his words ring as true as ever.

CHAPTER 3

What God Thinks of Cities

As part of his seminary internship, a 27-year-old student was sent to pastor an inner-city church so that, on weekends, he could participate in real-world ministry in addition to his studies during the week.

The largely Hispanic urban neighborhood he visited during his internship was very different from the countryside where he had grown up. As for the church itself, many members had already left for the suburbs. On his first Sunday, the young seminarian looked out from the pulpit and counted a total of 11 faces.

Imagine his further discouragement back on campus when he met a theologian who argued that conservative evangelicals, such as the seminarian, "could not survive in the city. To take the Bible literally is to become anti-urban. God's favorite people were shepherds; his next-favorite people were vine-growers and farmers; and his least favorite people were urban dwellers."

Thankfully, the young seminarian rejected this view, going on to become a veteran urban pastor. As he wrote, much later, of the anti-urban doctrines some believers embraced: "It was a concept I could not accept. We suffered in those early years, but I did not feel that God was driving us from the city; rather that we were being taught and refined by sharing in the city's pain."[6]

What Really Happened at Babel?

The notion that God frowns on city life has been around a long time, and the Scripture most often brought up to support this view is Genesis 11:1-9. A group of people aspired to "build ourselves a city, with a tower that reaches to heaven, so that we may make a name for ourselves; otherwise we will be scattered over the face of the whole earth" (verse 4). God, however, opted to derail this plan by confusing their language into many tongues, so that they could no longer understand each other.

The proper exegesis of this story must include remembering God's previous mandate to Adam's race: "Fill the earth and subdue it" (Genesis 1:28). He repeated much the same idea after the Flood (see Genesis 9:7). In those early times, God was most interested in populating the planet far and wide. (Some observers have noted that this divine command seems to be the only one we humans have thoroughly obeyed!)

> Some people cite Bible passages
> about Babel to demean cities, but in
> Revelation Scripture gives lavish
> portrayals of heaven in terms of a
> *city.*

The group at Babel didn't want to spread out; they wanted to stay in one place. More specifically, they wanted to build a "tower" in this one place. What kind of tower? More than a few Old Testament expositors have identified this as "a prototype ziggurat or temple-mound, first found in classical form early in the third millennium BC."[7] If indeed this was a place for worshiping pagan gods, no wonder God promptly put a stop to it.

Suffice it to say, little can be derived about cities from the Babel incident. Instead, it tells us mainly about people's failure to stay aligned with what God had ordained in that era. They made their plans while leaving God out of the equation.

The other pair of passages that sometimes draw anti-urban sentiment are the accounts of Jesus lamenting the hard-heartedness of Jerusalem to the point of tears (Luke 13:34-35 and 19:41-44). His indictments, however, are very specific to that particular city. Its people had stubbornly ignored His message of peace, just as they had mistreated previous Israelite prophets and failed to make their city a beacon of blessing to the nations (see Isaiah 2:1-4).

It would be a far stretch to say that this constitutes a blanket condemnation of urban living.

What Lies Ahead for Us All

In contrast, Scripture gives lavish portrayals of heaven in terms of a *city*. John, the Revelator, watches in amazement as a golden cube, measuring some 2,200 kilometers (1,400 miles) on each side, majestically comes "down out of heaven from God. It shone with the glory of God, and its brilliance was like that of a very precious jewel, like a jasper, clear as crystal" (Revelation 21:10-11).

John rhapsodizes at length about its gates, its walls, its bejeweled foundations, its round-the-clock illumination, its river of healing water. Overall, it was a stunning paradise. This is the pinnacle of God's provision for His people.

Some readers of the book of Genesis have tried to say that the Garden of Eden was perfection—and it's all gone downhill from there. But Revelation 21-22 tells us there will be a second, even more glorious perfection—in the form of a city. Eternity will not be a scene where each of us gets our own farm. Instead, we will move into a marvelous city alongside the One who is the eternal light.

That prospect is referenced throughout the pages of Scripture. For example: Abraham, though he lived many years as a nomad, is said to have been "looking forward to the city with foundations, whose architect and builder is God" (Hebrews 11:10). Other saints mentioned in that same chapter, though "foreigners and strangers on earth," are honored as "longing for a better country—a heavenly one. Therefore God is not ashamed to be called their God, for *he has prepared a city for them*" (verse 16, italics added).

Near the end of Hebrews, the author bears the same witness regarding himself: "For here we do not have an enduring city, but we are looking for the city that is to come" (13:14). The glories of heaven are undeniably urban glories.

An Urban Roll Call

Before we arrive on those celestial streets, however, we live with the complex realities of own earthly cities. And so have God's people for centuries. The Scriptures, time and again, show God caring about city dwellers, not pushing them away. He has always recognized the value of cities and incorporated them into His mission for us.

Let's take a look at some of the people and places that give us a better understanding of God's deep love for cities and the people who live there.

Jonah. God directed him to take a divine message to what he called "the great city of Nineveh" (Jonah 4:11), a capital in the ancient world. When Jonah resisted, God employed extreme measures to get his compliance! He would not let the prophet ignore the urban need.

To Jonah's great surprise, the city dwellers responded positively. The king "took off his royal robes, covered himself with sackcloth and sat down in the dust" (3:6). He then issued a proclamation for all his subjects to do the same, saying, "Let everyone call urgently on God. Let them give up their evil ways and their violence. Who knows? God may yet relent and with compassion turn from his fierce anger so that we will not perish" (3:8, 9).

Talk about revival in the city! God was, no doubt, smiling at the whole outcome.

Isaiah. This prophet's account of a prediction God had given him (Isaiah chapter 26) is familiar to us because of verse 3 ("Thou will keep him in perfect peace"—KJV) that is so often quoted by modern Christians. But upon closer inspection, we find that the setting of this verse shows God's loving attention to a city:

In that day this song will be sung in the land of Judah:

We have a strong city;
God makes salvation
its walls and ramparts.
Open the gates
that the righteous nation may enter,

the nation that keeps faith.
You will keep in perfect peace
   those whose minds are steadfast,
   because they trust in you.
Trust in the LORD forever,
   for the LORD, the LORD himself, is the Rock eternal (verses 1-4).

God is not interested in urban decay. He wants cities to be "strong" places where righteousness can thrive.

A few chapters later, we hear this passionate plea to the residents of the Israelite capital not to give in to despair:

People of Zion, who live in Jerusalem, you will weep no more. How gracious he will be when you cry for help! As soon as he hears, he will answer you. Although the Lord gives you the bread of adversity and the water of affliction, your teachers will be hidden no more; with your own eyes you will see them. Whether you turn to the right or to the left, your ears will hear a voice behind you, saying, "This is the way; walk in it" (Isaiah 30:19-21).

Again, this final sentence has been extracted from the text by modern Christians as a promise of personal guidance in decision making. Perhaps that is warranted. But let it also be suggested that perhaps the "way" God is quietly whispering for us to walk is the boulevards and avenues of today's cities.

More than a hundred years after Isaiah's time, the people of Judah were finally being judged for their waywardness and were—to their shock—taken into exile. They had never, in their worst nightmares, imagined such a calamity. But it had come to pass.

Jeremiah. Amidst these dire circumstances of exile, the prophet Jeremiah wrote a letter on how to go on living. He did not wallow in despair. He did not tell them simply to huddle together and endure the 70 years of punishment. Instead, he had better ideas:

This is what the LORD Almighty, the God of Israel, says to all those I carried into exile from Jerusalem to Babylon: "Build houses and settle down; plant gardens and eat what they produce. Marry and have sons and daughters; find wives for your sons and give your daughters in marriage, so that they too may

have sons and daughters. Increase in number there; do not decrease. Also, seek
the peace and prosperity of the city to which I have carried you into exile.
Pray to the Lord for it, because if it prospers, you too will prosper" (Jeremiah
29:4-7).

The message could not be clearer: Get involved in the city where you find
yourselves! Work for the common good. Pray for positive things to happen.

We who find ourselves in urban centers today should do no less, because
this is the obvious will of our God. Later in this book, we will cite multiple
examples of Christians doing exactly what this text describes.

In the New Testament era, we see the people of "The Way" following an
urban-focused strategy. We read letters to healthy, established churches in
places such as Rome, the capital of the empire; Philippi, "a Roman colony and
the leading city of that district" (Acts 16:12); Corinth, a major transit point for
east-west commerce. Christian congregations were vibrant in all these places.

Antioch. The third largest city in the empire attracted Christians when
persecution in Jerusalem grew intense and caused believers to relocate to
other cities.

Antioch "boasted a fine seaport" and "was renowned for its culture, being
commended in this respect by no less a person than Cicero."[8] The population was notably multicultural—and so was the wise and effective leadership
group in the church (see Acts 13:1-2).

This became the first mission-minded church, sending out missionaries
such as Paul and his associates multiple times. No doubt the presence of various ethnicities and skin colors in their midst made them especially alert to
the spiritual needs of people everywhere (unlike the Jerusalem church, which
had real problems with discrimination on the basis of language; see Acts 6).

The example of Antioch gives us a lesson for our time, namely, that any
church that doesn't think multi-culturally is going to have a tough time in
the city, because most big cities are a real mixture of people. We may posit a
general rule: *If you're going to minister in an urban area, you are going to have
to relate across cultural lines, like the Antioch Christians did.*

Paul. The Christian pastor and evangelist naturally understood the importance of urban ministry. He had grown up in Tarsus, a city estimated to be "no

less than half a million in Roman times."⁹ Thus, its citizens enjoyed the advantage of full Roman citizenship—which Paul used to his advantage more than once. Much of his advanced education was acquired in Jerusalem, another important city. Once Paul began his traveling ministry, we cannot help noticing how he centered on major cities, even though the empire was overwhelmingly rural in this time.

Ephesus. Paul was an itinerant missionary before he settled down for more than two years in this strong export hub, which was home to the infamous temple of the goddess Diana/Artemis (the temple was four times as large as the Parthenon in Athens).

Paul was not intimidated by this in the least; he "spoke boldly there … arguing persuasively about the kingdom of God" (Acts 19:8). He led daily discussions in a lecture hall. He worked mighty miracles, sometimes even at a distance through the use of "handkerchiefs and aprons that had touched him" (verse 12).

As a result, the light of the gospel moved out in concentric circles toward the countryside. The biblical summary of his time in Ephesus: "All the Jews and Greeks who lived in the province of Asia heard the word of the Lord" (verse 10).

This is a demonstration of how important cities are. They carry huge influence. If we can make the gospel take root in a major city, it affects people well into the rural areas.

Throughout both Old and New Testaments, God repeatedly shows His favor on those who take His light into cities. He is eager to maximize the urban dynamic for extending His rule in the world. Far from being negative about cities, God sees great potential for their influence. And so should we.

PART TWO:
EIGHT CRITICAL RESPONSES

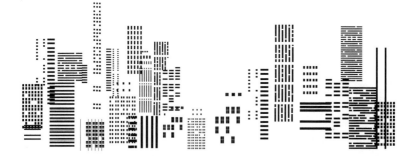

CHAPTER 4

Action 1: Pray Together

You may be tempted to skip this chapter so you can get on to newer, fresher, more innovative ideas for urban ministry.

Please don't.

Of course, we all believe in praying; we talk about it all the time. No Christian would ever breathe the heresy that prayer is unimportant or peripheral.

But actually doing the work of prayer (by ourselves or with others) is a different matter. It is not hard to say, "Let's open this meeting with a word of prayer," or "Yes, my friend, I'll pray for you." However, actually investing time in talking with God is not something that happens as often as our words might indicate.

Kingdom work in the metacities (today's largest cities, far larger than megacities) of the 21st century is more dependent upon prayer than any sophisticated strategy or formula. The words of Psalm 127:1 echo at the edges of our conference rooms: "Unless the LORD builds the house, the builders labor in vain. Unless the LORD watches over the city, the guards stand watch in vain."

The best-laid campaigns and charts will fall short without divine empowerment. Samuel Chadwick (1860-1932), a Methodist leader and college president, said it well: "The work of God is not by might of men or by the power of men but by his Spirit. It is by Him the truth convicts and converts, sanctifies and saves. The philosophies of men fail, but the Word of God in the demonstration of the Spirit prevails."[10]

Therefore, it is vital that Christian leaders from all ethnic and denominational backgrounds come together to pray for their cities and for one another. As they plead with God for an effective witness in their setting, breakthroughs start to happen.

Why Urban Ministry Demands Prayer

There are at least three reasons for calling upon God together.

1) It Can Be Tough in the City

Anyone who has worked in city ministry for very long knows that cities can be tough environments. The powers of evil are arrayed on all sides, from hostile civic authorities to people's personal bondages to the literal forces of hell. This is no easy road.

Pastor Jim Cymbala tells in his book *Fresh Wind, Fresh Fire* about a desperate afternoon early in his ministry at a tiny, dysfunctional church called the Brooklyn Tabernacle, when he bemoaned to God:

> "Lord, I have no idea how to be a successful pastor.... I haven't been trained. All I know is that Carol [his wife] and I are working in the middle of New York City, with people dying on every side, overdosing from heroin, consumed by materialism, and all the rest. If the gospel is so powerful ..."
>
> I couldn't finish the sentence. Tears choked me....
>
> Then quietly but forcefully, in words heard not with my ear but deep within my spirit, I sensed God speaking:
>
> *If you and your wife will lead my people to pray and call upon my name, you will never lack for something fresh to preach. I will supply all the money that's needed, both for the church and for your family, and you will never have a building large enough to contain the crowds I will send in response.*
>
> I was overwhelmed. My tears intensified.... I knew I had heard from God.[11]

He returned to his pulpit the next Sunday and made the shocking announcement that, as of that moment, the Tuesday night prayer meeting would be "the barometer of our church. What happens on Tuesday night will be the gauge by which we will judge success or failure, because that will be the measure by which God blesses us."

Today, if you visit this 3,400-seat church in downtown Brooklyn on a Tuesday night, you will find several thousand people fervently calling out to God for His help. They intercede for desperately needed jobs, for unsaved relatives, for wayward children, for physical healing, for safety in the perilous streets and subways, for outreaches to the needy. There is little preaching, no formalities, and no music from the award-winning Brooklyn Tabernacle Choir (which sings on Sundays). Instead, it is all about prayer.

> The family of God, in nearly every city, is notoriously divided by history, doctrinal interpretations, ethnic diversity, and even individual personalities.

In the Gospel of Mark, when nine of Jesus' disciples faced a particularly difficult stronghold of Satan at the foot of the mountain—a pitiful boy tormented by seizures—they tried to cast out the demon but failed. Later, they asked their Master why. His answer: "This kind can come out only by prayer" (Mark 9:29).

Be warned: the various demons we face in modern cities are just as hard to dislodge.

2) Breaking Down the Walls

A second reason we need to pray to God about the cities of our world is because we need to break down the walls of division between us. The family of God in nearly every city is notoriously divided by history, doctrinal interpretations, ethnic diversity, and even individual personalities. Working together to advance the Kingdom does not come naturally. Too often, we are preoccupied with our own labels.

The unbelievers, of course, could not care less about our denominational or theological labels. In fact, they find them rather mystifying. For us to lift up Christ and Christ alone will require a change in our mindset. This change is best accomplished on our knees—together.

In recent years, the Council of Pastors in Buenos Aires, Argentina (pop. 2.9 million), has been giving us a worthy example. "Each time the New Testament speaks of the church in a city such as Ephesus, it is always singular, never plural," a Baptist pastor named Carlos Mraida told *Christianity Today* magazine. "Yet when the New Testament speaks of leadership in a city, it is always plural. The church is singular, but the leadership is plural."

One of his fellow pastors, Norberto Saracco of Good News Church, continued with a poignant observation. "When we go to the U.S., we cannot understand the division of the church. You can have one pastor on one [street] corner and another on another corner, and they don't know each other. Here we are friends."[12]

As a result, this council of some 180 pastors meets regularly to support each other, share resources (even money), plan joint projects, and pray together. In 2008 they organized 40 days of prayer, ending with an outdoor vigil for three nights in front of the nation's Congress. This entire capital is taking notice of the gospel—and responding to it.

The pastors speak of their efforts as long-term, not just an event. "Unity of the city is a process," says Mraida.

We across the Body of Christ may never agree on such doctrinal matters as predestination or the timing of the Second Coming. We may not preach from the same lectionary or with the same style. We probably don't worship with the same music. But at least we can *pray* together. And when we do, the God and Father of us all is listening.

3) Tuning in to God

A third reason we need to pray is because we need to tune ourselves to the will of God. Prayer gets us beyond "what I think" and "what strategy I propose" and tunes our ear to what God is thinking and directing. It reminds us that there is, indeed, a "Lord of the harvest" (Matthew 9:38)—and it's not us. The workers He seeks to employ must be aligned with Him.

In Ghana, when the "New Life for All" movement was just starting, in the mid-1970s, to seek to evangelize the entire country on an planned basis, one of the first things missionary Ross Campbell and his colleagues did was to hold three-day retreats for pastors and other church leaders. More than 120 of these events were conducted. One result, not entirely expected, was that the gatherings helped many pastors return to a living faith! They had been nominal Christians, of course, but they were hardly energized by the power of the gospel. Now, after praying with others for three days, their whole perspective was changed.

Campbell firmly believed that trying to enthuse unconverted ministers with largely unconverted congregations to go out and bring the unconverted to Christ would be doomed to failure. The act of praying together dealt with that issue at the front; then true evangelism could begin.

All kinds of strategies followed in the wake of these prayer retreats for leaders. Prayer cells in local churches were begun; Bible study outlines and witnessing aids were circulated; pastors selected key lay leaders to equip and involve congregational members in lifestyle evangelism; measurable goals were enacted. The entire Ghanaian church seemed energized.

And what was the result? "The number of Protestant churches [at the start was] 10,105 in 1976. In the decade 1977-86, a further 8,575 new congregations were established—a growth of 85 percent."[13] The power of prayer had activated remarkable progress for the Kingdom in a relatively short amount of time.

How Large? How Small?

The formats for praying together may vary widely. Some gatherings may be huge, drawing public attention. On one occasion, in Cape Town, South Africa, more than 45,000 Christians packed into Newlands Rugby Stadium for a "Day of Remembrance and Prayer." It went so well that by the next year, similar prayer gatherings were held in eight different provinces across the nation.

Stories could be told of comparable events in some of the large cities of Asia and the Pacific, Latin America, North America, and Europe. Various prayer movement organizations have sprung up to encourage the church to call upon God out in the open, where all can see (especially on Pentecost Sunday each year).

But huge assemblies are not the only way. Some engage in "prayer walks" through or around cities, asking God to visit each neighborhood and business district they see. Others hold prayer retreats and all-night prayer meetings. I remember being in a Brazilian hotel once and opening the window late on a Friday night, only to hear the sounds of nearby churches interceding for their city.

Many churches across the world (including the Brooklyn Tabernacle mentioned above) have set up a prayer team that meets in a separate room *during* the Sunday services. These people fervently call upon God to touch needy hearts through the preaching of the Word so that a spiritual harvest can be reaped that day.

The number of those who pray is not the point, whether an arena-full or "where two or three are gathered together" (Matthew 18:20). God has promised to hear whenever His people seek His face, admitting that human effort alone cannot meet the challenges of a broken world.

Jolted to Act

I will always be grateful that when I first began mission work as an ambitious young graduate from England, I came under the tutorship of a man who took prayer seriously. Hans von Staden, whom I introduced in chapter one, had been profoundly moved a few years earlier by reading the works of a great South African man of God, Andrew Murray (1828-1917).

Murray had been invited to come speak at the Ecumenical Missionary Conference in April, 1900, in New York. But he felt disinclined to make the long trip due to the outbreak of the Second Boer War in his homeland. Later on, when Murray read the published proceedings of the conference, he was disturbed at one glaring omission. Speakers had waxed eloquent on the need for pastors and seminaries to lift up the missions cause, for more and better missions literature to be published, for more funds to be raised, and so forth— but almost nothing had been said about prayer!

So Murray wrote a book entitled *The Key to the Missionary Problem* (1902).

In the final chapters he challenged global Christendom to set up "Weeks of Prayer" for the world:

> There can be no more urgent duty resting upon the Church than to give itself to prayer, first of all, that its members at home may be roused and sanctified to take their part in the struggle with the hosts of darkness, 'praying with all prayer and supplication in the Spirit.' ... Those who know what prayer is must only pray and labour the more earnestly that the life of Christians may be so deepened by the Holy Ghost, that it shall become 'as natural and easy to pray daily for foreign missions as to pray for daily bread.'

Sixty years later, Hans von Staden read this and was jolted. He determined that the Dorothea Mission must take up this call.

And so when I arrived, one of my first assignments was to set up a Week of Prayer in Umtata, the capital of the Transkei (now part of Eastern Cape Province). A few months later, I was doing the same thing in Nairobi, the capital of Kenya. The format was intensive; we called Christians to give six full days for prayer, gathering at 7:00 a.m., then again at 9:00 a.m., 11:00 a.m., 3:00 p.m., and finally at 7:00 p.m.

> Huge assemblies are not the only way to reach urbanites. Some teams engage in "prayer walks" through or around cities, asking God to visit each neighborhood and business district they see.

For these prayer events, I made two very large maps—one of Africa (six feet by eight feet), the other of the whole world (twelve feet by ten feet), showing the countries and religious majorities in each. Generally, a knowledgeable speaker would begin each session by sharing prayer needs; then we would get down to praying for at least two thirds of the allotted time.

To help focus on international needs beyond Africa, I also began compiling a list of nations and as much information as I could gather. The first booklet was only 30 or so pages. But it was the beginning of what grew into *Operation World*, published today in its seventh edition as "the definitive prayer guide to every nation."

Today, *Operation World* runs 978 pages long. Nearly three million copies of the successive editions have been printed. (See www.operationworld.org for ways to purchase.) To this day, I am amazed and gratified to keep meeting full-time missionaries all over the world who trace their ministry call or their field of service back to reading this resource.

You might think that a whole week of prayer would grow tedious, even exhausting. Actually, many people expressed astonishment at how quickly the time went. Sometimes we broke up into small groups or even pairs, but more often we prayed corporately as a larger body. We sought, as much as possible, to agree on specific prayer targets and then "pray through" until we were sure God had heard. Then we could move along to praise and thanksgiving.

As my colleagues and I kept arranging more and more Weeks of Prayer, we were sometimes able to meet in a secluded or retreat site. But other times, we stayed in the city and used a church, a conference center, or one of Dorothea Mission's large evangelistic tents. The format eventually spread beyond Africa to various European countries. It was a moving experience to be in such gatherings with so many people (sometimes more than a hundred at a time) praying for a lost world.

And in every place, the passion of Hans von Staden was echoed. I can still hear him saying, "When man works, man works; when man prays, God works." Another watchword of his was this:

Much prayer, much blessing;

Little prayer, little blessing;

No prayer, no blessing.

Did it do any Good?

And blessings we did receive, in undeniable ways. For example, we organized a Week of Prayer in Beira, the second largest city of Mozambique, in 1965, to beseech God to break open that nation for the gospel. At the time, Portugal and its colonial empire was ruled by an ardently Catholic dictator, so that Protestant mission activity was limited or even forbidden.

While the south part of the country had a number of churches because of Mozambican miners who had received the gospel in South Africa and then had come home, the center and north regions were only partially evangelized—and under serious persecution. Eddie and Alice Cain, who served with WEC (World Evangelization for Christ), had long prayed to enter this land but had been refused visas.

We met in beach huts that week. The secret police watched us closely each day. But they left us alone to continue our intercession.

And God heard. Within a few months, the Cains got their visas, moved into the capital, and began to minister. They made spiritual headway for at least a decade, until in 1975, the Communist Frelimo nationalists gained power and cracked down on all Christian ministries. While that influence waned over time, in recent years, Mozambique has been one of the most receptive lands for the gospel. How much of all this was due to the weeks of prayer?

Three other praises may be noted:

- We prayed in many places about a better future for South Africa and pled with God to soften hard hearts and bring reconciliation to this important nation. It was indeed a miracle in the early 1990s when apartheid finally collapsed—without a shot being fired.

- On an intercontinental level, we prayed fervently during the 1970s and '80s for the USSR and its client states. Everything looked dark during those years. And then ... the Berlin Wall suddenly came down, the Soviet Union split up into 16 separate countries, and Kingdom workers were able to do things for God that they had only dreamed about. Again, all this happened without a war.

- We prayed much for Muslim lands to open to the gospel. Most of them were considered "closed," with only a few (even clandestine) Christian workers. In the 1960s, there were probably fewer than 100,000 believers from a Muslim background (BMBs). Today we reckon there are between 7 and 17 million BMBs, mostly in the cities of the Middle East and North Africa. The numbers of church planters and disciple-makers is estimated to be somewhere around 16,000. From Algeria all the way to Indonesia, we are seeing mass movements of people toward Christ.

Again, how much of this is in direct answer to prayer?

Prayer—bold, insistent prayer—faith-filled prayer—persistent, determined prayer—is key to seeing the powers of darkness repelled and the light of Christ exalted. We must never become too sophisticated to bow down in intercession for the cities of our world.

ASK YOURSELF

- *Do I have a specific list of prayer items regarding city ministry that gets deeper than just "Lord, bless the work"?*
- *If not, what should go onto such a list?*
- *Who do I know who would be willing to pray with me about these needs? (Write down their names.)*
- *How might I organize prayer times for such a group?*
- *What place does intercessory prayer for the unevangelized world hold in the life of my church? What can be done to improve this?*

CHAPTER 5

Action 2: Exegete the City

Our Father God to whom we pray knows every street, every block, every home, and even every person living in the sprawling urban centers of our world. Census takers may try to record the ethnic heritages, languages spoken, number of bathrooms or television sets, amount of household income, and much more—but God already knows it all.

The problem is: we don't.

If we have visited a particular city multiple times, or especially if we reside in a certain sector of the city, we may think we know it well. We can find our way around without a map. The names of avenues, parks, schools, and government buildings are familiar to us. We may even call this city "home."

But there is much more to learn. Many aspects of the city remain to be explored.

Those who seek to do God's work in a city must operate out of knowledge, not assumption. The need for research is critical. Otherwise, we may miss important pockets of opportunity.

As the ever-quotable Ray Bakke says about his ministry in Chicago, "I needed to know the city, because if you don't know it, you can't love it." He has often compared this study to the work a pastor invests in preparing a sermon. Seminaries and Bible colleges teach how to exegete a passage of Scripture so that the Word of God is handled accurately. In a parallel way, Kingdom workers must "exegete the city" to which God has called them.

The goal is not just to collect piles of numbers and charts. The goal is to highlight unreached sections and areas of the city population, which then motivates workers and churches to specific action.

Who Lives Where

In recent years, notable Christian research has been done in such major cities as Mexico City, Lima (Peru), Nairobi (Kenya), and Singapore. When the "New Life for All" campaign was taking shape in Ghana (mentioned earlier), the committee invested considerable effort and time in studying not only the capital city of Accra, but the outlying areas as well. They sought to know such things as:

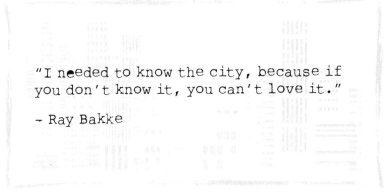

"I needed to know the city, because if you don't know it, you can't love it."

— Ray Bakke

- How much progress had been made in establishing an active, witnessing church in every village, town, neighborhood, and minority community?
- What is the location of every existing church, and how fast it was growing and multiplying?
- What places are yet to be evangelized?
- What facts can help to set realistic goals for church planting?

"Armed with questionnaires for the churches and localities, the GEC [Ghana Evangelism Committee] staff, assisted by church leaders, visited virtually every town and village of 50 or more people region by region. Thousands of kilometers were covered by car, motorbike, pushbike, canoe, and on foot to complete a survey of every church and every locality. They came back with the facts, which were then carefully compiled and published.

"For the discerning church leader, the published surveys provide[d] a gold mine of information. They [swept] away the fog and the false assumptions accumulated over years by [merely] promotional church reporting."[14]

In other words, the research dug down beneath the level of inspiring stories and human-interest anecdotes in order to map what had really been accomplished so far—and what was still waiting to be done. The differences between southern Ghana's more churchgoing (or at least church-belonging) population and northern Ghana's more tribal followers of traditional religions was plain for all to see and study.

According to one of the organizers, the result was "a great challenge to our complacency, and a call for urgent and serious prayer, consideration and action." In fact, many churches were energized, stagnant denominations began growing again, and the planting of new churches multiplied.

Digging Deeper

A more city-specific example comes from the "Twin Cities" of Minneapolis and St. Paul, Minnesota, USA (population 3.5 million). Long considered to be the center of Scandinavian immigrants who started coming to America more than a hundred years ago, many people still bear such Nordic surnames as Lundquist and Cedarberg and Carlson (or Carlsen, or Karlsson, or …). An impressive museum called the American Swedish Institute draws 100,000 visitors every year. The professional football team is called the Minnesota Vikings.

But for the past few decades, a local group called City Vision (www.cityvisiontc.org) has been looking deeper. A series of eye-opening reports have been published, the 16th edition (release date February 2015) being the latest. Page after page of attractive charts and lists tell the true story of the Twin Cities.

For example, the University of Minnesota, in Minneapolis, has the largest number of Chinese students of any American university. Imagine the surprise when blond-haired, blue-eyed church folk first learned that the Twin Cities are home to 77,000 Somalis—the highest concentration of any U.S. city. Nearly all of them are Muslims.

The city also includes some 40,000 Native Americans (commonly called "Indians"), only 1 percent of whom attend church.

Sikhs from South Asia have managed to set up a Sikh temple—in a former church building. In fact, ten different church buildings built years ago (no doubt by Scandinavian craftsmen) are now mosques.

Religious Climate of the Twin Cities

Religious Climate

Religious Identification	Number of Adherents in the Twin Cities	Percent of Twin Cities Population
Cult/Sect/Occult	117,200	3%
World Religions	337,000	10%
Non–Evangelical Christians	563,315	16%
Evangelical Christians	1,135,965	33%
Unchurched or Nominal Christians	1,305,666	38%

Twin Cities Religious Distribution Based on Attendance

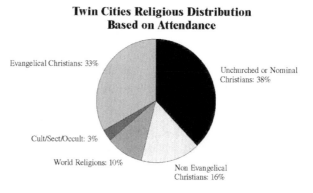

Evangelical Christians: 33%

Unchurched or Nominal Christians: 38%

Cult/Sect/Occult: 3%

World Religions: 10%

Non Evangelical Christians: 16%

From *Cityview Report* by John A. Mayer. Used by permission.

Most surprising, the metroplex is home to 20,000 witches and 288 witch covens, plus a large occult publishing company, leading some to call the Twin Cities "Paganistan." One coven even meets in a church. In the 2006 election, a witch ran for governor of the state.

It is amazing that all of this is happening in a metro area that is home to as many as ten Christian colleges (including evangelical stalwarts Bethel, Northwestern, North Central, and Crown) and was, for decades, the headquarters of the Billy Graham Evangelistic Association.

To further show the diversity and change that's happening in Minneapolis, along one route, the LRT (Light Rail Transit system) sells tickets in four languages—English, Spanish, Hmong, and Somali. Not far away, a six-block stretch along Nicollet Avenue has 75 ethnic restaurants, from Vietnamese to Caribbean and has been dubbed "Eat Street." There you can buy food products including yak, kangaroo, guinea pig, goat, and even goat milk lollipops.

To make all this diversity real, City Vision began offering day-long Discover Your City tours for pastors, church planters, lay leaders, students, and anyone else interested in seeing the mission needs right on their doorstep. Stops along the way include ethnic stores and tastes—sipping Somali tea at a Somali mall or having a camel burger. More than 18,000 people have taken these tours.

This kind of "street exegesis" has led congregations and individuals to ask what they might do to share the Good News with these neighbors. One answer has been sports outreach—forming soccer, basketball, and volleyball leagues for immigrant young people. Such activity doesn't require a lot of language proficiency since kids naturally gravitate toward anything that involves a ball.

Others have given away copies of the *Jesus* film in appropriate languages. As the result of two planning conferences that City Vision led, the first Somali church in America has been planted.

Not every venture has been successful, of course. One well-meaning church tried to reach out to its Somali neighborhood by planning free hot-dog lunches on Fridays. Despite good publicity and organization, nobody showed up. Disappointed, the church asked City Vision's executive director, Dr. John Mayer, what had gone wrong. He explained that (1) Muslims do not eat pork in any form, (2) Friday is the Muslim holy day, with prayers at the mosque beginning at noon, and (3) large-group gatherings are not as comfortable for newcomers as one-to-one relationships.

But other churches have made solid gains in representing Christ in the Twin Cities. One large church in a southwest suburb has planted ten other churches using City Vision data.

"What we do," says Dr. Mayer, "is like the twelve spies being sent by Moses to investigate the land of Canaan. We gather information on what our city is really like, then come back to God's people with reports. And like Joshua and Caleb, we encourage them to go up with courage and expectation."

A New Shortcut

Not every city's Kingdom workers will have the personnel and funding to do as much as the Twin Cities research group is doing, of course. But their example shows the right questions to pursue.

A new tactic that gets to some of the same information much faster has opened up thanks to Facebook and its Graph Search tool. As is well known, the Facebook "nation" is now the world's third largest community, with more than 1.2 *billion* users. It is especially popular among diasporas, as newly relocated people strive to find others like themselves in the new place—and also to stay in contact with what is happening "back home." Plus, it is free.

Of course, Facebook users are not shy to reveal all manner of detail in their "About" (personal profile) section—where they were born, what schools they attended, what languages they speak, what religion they follow, what politics they advocate, etc. None of this information has been forced out of them—they (we) freely volunteer it.

Now, using Graph Search, it takes only a few keystrokes to collect this information for a specific geography. For example, suppose you wish to reach out to Pakistanis living in London or Cambodians living in Sydney. It is a simple matter to query "Urdu speakers London" or "Khmer speakers Sydney." The results will tell you not only the size of the Facebook population but even individual names! Again, this is not some kind of Big Brother intrusion into people's privacy; it is only collecting what they themselves have chosen to share.

Trevor Castor, assistant director of the Zwemer Center for Muslim Studies (Columbia International University), has explored how Graph Search works.

He presented a paper on "Mapping the Diaspora with Facebook" at a 2014 meeting of the Evangelical Missiological Society (http://www.ciu.edu/news-story/rankin-and-castor-address-ems). At the time this book was going to press, Castor's paper was soon to be posted on the Zwemer Center website. (www.zwemercenter.com)

The Big Picture

Finally, for the overall view of the mission challenge around the world, I would refer you to the 240-page book I created (with much assistance from others) entitled *The Future of the Global Church—History, Trends and Possibilities.*

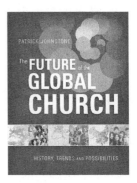

Published in 2011 by Biblica, Inc., and then InterVarsity Press (USA), it arose from two desires of mine—the first was to step back from my years of research for *Operation World* and try to understand what trends were discernible and how these trends indicate what future ministry might be like. The second was that I also might hand over some of my public speaking about the world and preparing the graphics in a replicable format that others could use in their public ministry.

The book is highly graphic in its presentation. In fact, there are more than 1,000 animated PowerPoint slides made available by GMI on the websites they manage, including the site www.thefutureoftheglobalchurch.org.

Through all of this, the reader can quickly see the realities of our world's spiritual condition. The exegesis of our planet clarifies what is actually factual, not just what we've imagined. From this point, it is but a matter for all of us to ask the poignant question attributed to Saul of Tarsus on the Damascus Road, "Lord, what will you have me to do?"

And how did Jesus reply? "Now get up and go into the city" (Acts 9:6).

ASK YOURSELF

- *What do I wish I knew about my city and its spiritual needs?*
- *What kinds of research is already available? Where could I access it?*
- *What original research might I do that would be helpful without costing a fortune?*
- *Who is already researching my city, and how could I be involved? If no one is doing this, what could I initiate, and who could help me?*
- *Once I gather the information, how would I disseminate it to other Kingdom workers of like mind?*

CHAPTER 6

Action 3:
Push Against Urban Poverty

Once we know, through research, what is actually going on in a given city, we immediately realize that grinding, gnawing poverty is fully alive. The tall skyscrapers and polished airport terminals do not tell the whole story of any metropolis. Indeed, the people who clean those skyscraper offices and push luggage carts for inbound tourists may be wondering where their next meal will come from, even as they work. Is there truly a God who cares about their distress?

Careful studies by the United Nations tell us that despite all the efforts of governments, secular charities, and even churches, to alleviate poverty, the proportion of those living on the edge will stubbornly remain the same over the next 40 years, as shown in the chart on the next page.

("EuNAPa" stands for Europe, North America, and the Pacific nations; "AfAsLA" stands for Africa, Asia, and Latin America.)

Notice that the striped band is as wide on one side of the chart as on the other—approximately 2 billion men, women, and children. To bring this down to local terms that can be visualized, 66 percent of the 14 million people who call Kolkata, India, home are families living in just one room.

Across the world, people with money get tired of thinking about this massive issue. Fatigue among the "haves" is entirely understandable. Too many

Christians are prone to throw up their hands and turn away, snatching a half-sentence from Jesus: "The poor you will always have with you ..." (Mark 14:7).

The global distribution of city- and slum-dwellers, 1950–2050

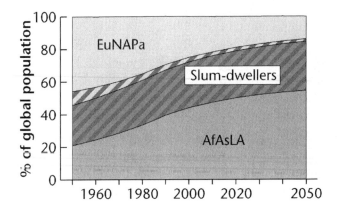

Let it be clearly noticed that Jesus immediately continued His sentence with "... and you can help them any time you want." He, the Man who was Himself homeless with no earthly goods beyond what He could carry, should never be cited on the side of lethargy or unconcern. What He said that day was in some ways an echo from the words of Moses, who was even more direct: "There will always be poor people in the land. Therefore I command you to be openhanded toward your fellow Israelites who are poor and needy" (Deuteronomy 15:11).

The apostle James was equally blunt when he wrote: "Suppose a brother or a sister is without clothes and daily food. If one of you says to them, 'Go in peace; keep warm and well fed,' but does nothing about their physical needs, what good is it? In the same way, faith by itself, if it is not accompanied by action, is dead" (James 2:15-17).

According to Ash Barker, the Australian who founded Urban Neighbors of Hope (UNOH) and who lived for more than a decade with the poor of Bangkok, one of six people on our planet live in an urban slum—but only one out of 500 Christian missionaries actually work there.

We can do better than this.

A Variety of Methods

The models for ministry to the poor are varied, and one is not necessarily better than another. In fact, they can easily integrate with each other, depending on time, place, need, and resources available. Nevertheless, here is a list (doubtless incomplete) of current strategies.

1) Give straightforward aid, especially in the aftermath of trauma.

When a typhoon slams inland from an angry ocean, when rains don't come, causing crops to fail and food prices to soar, when marauding armies or terrorists run roughshod over a helpless civilian population, it is entirely fitting for those who carry the name of Christ to step forward. The sooner that food, clothing, and temporary shelter can be put in place, the better.

The precedent for this kind of ministry goes, at least, back to New Testament times. When the Antioch church learned, through the prophet Agabus, that "a severe famine would spread over the entire Roman world…the disciples, as each was able, decided to provide help for the brothers and sisters living in Judea" (Acts 11:28-29). Some years later, the apostle Paul again raised funds from the Macedonian and Achaian churches to relieve another food crisis (see 2 Corinthians 8-9). In urging generosity, he quoted Psalm 112:9, "They have freely scattered their gifts to the poor; their righteousness endures forever."

Christian mechanisms are continuing this kind of work in our day. Tearfund (U.K) is one example. Hilfe für die Brüder (Germany) is another. For a North American list, see the Accord Network (www.accordnetwork.org), which has some 60 members, from the Salvation Army to World Concern to a number of denominational agencies.

2) Empower the poor toward self-sufficiency.

Many of the same ministries work to train, coach, and even sometimes capitalize those in need so they can begin to earn their own living. Extending microloans to get a business started is one way. While some secular and government programs have succumbed to greed by charging exorbitant interest rates, Christian agencies in this field—Opportunity International, Hope International, among others—have kept their focus on serving the poor above all else. (See "Staying on Mission," *Christianity Today,* May 2011, pp. 23-25).

And the need is larger than just money. One group, Mission India, is focusing on helping local churches start literacy classes for those in need, particularly Indian women, one-third of whom cannot read or write.

"People who are illiterate get cheated in the marketplace," says David Stravers, president. "You read about the growing Indian economy, its growing middle class, its high-tech industry—but it also has heavy inflation. If you're illiterate and your wages are stuck at one dollar a day, which is very common, that only hurts you." For a Christian church to teach you to read is a huge empowerment in the modern environment.

3) Hold public events that feed body and soul.

Some ministries have sprung up to help the urban poor through high-profile community days of sharing free food, medical and dental screening, job placement assistance, entertainment for the children—and the gospel. One such organization is Convoy of Hope (www.convoyofhope.org), now active in 44 countries on five continents. Brightly painted trucks roll in to an open parking lot or field, colorful tents are set up, and swarms of people come to see what's taking place. Soon the gates open, and the festivities begin. A central stage features the message of Christ both in music and speaking. As a result, families go home not only with groceries but also with a new understanding of God's grace.

4) Make a long-term investment in the next generation.

On the opposite end of the time scale, some ministries commit years to developing the children of a poor community to be leaders for the future. The mechanism is child sponsorship—a modest monthly donation from a faraway "sponsor" that guarantees school tuition, medical attention, and at least one solid meal per day. While generic and secular programs also use this model, the openly Christian ones often partner with a loving local church that welcomes the child each week, provides tutoring if needed, and gives encouragement. Meanwhile, the sponsor prays for the child and sends occasional letters. One of the strongest such programs is Compassion International; its slogan says it well: "Releasing children from poverty in Jesus' name."

Currently more than a million children are being sponsored through Compassion across 26 nations, from Burkina Faso to El Salvador to Sri Lanka. As many as 80,000 of them make personal commitments to Christ each year. Dr. Wess Stafford, who grew up himself as a missionary child in Ivory Coast and served as Compassion president for 20 years, was famous for assuring children wherever he met them, "You may have been born into poverty—but poverty was not born into you." Indeed, sponsored children have risen up out of the slums to become doctors, educators, and political leaders in their countries. Whole nations whose children used to receive aid have now become donor nations instead (example: South Korea).

> The precedent for emergency aid to city dwellers who suffer goes back 2,000 years to the time when the Antioch church learned through the prophet Agabus that famine would spread over the entire Roman world.

5) Become an actual neighbor of the poor.

On a whole different level are those who actually move into a slum for an extended period—even years—in order to embody the gospel. They swelter in the same heat, buy food in the same open-air markets, fight off the same rats, and try to sleep through the same sirens at night.

These are what Scott Bessenecker, associate director of missions with Inter-Varsity Christian Fellowship, calls "the New Friars," after St. Francis of Assisi and others who renounced wealth and privilege to live among the poor.[15]

Three Basic Steps

New Zealander Dr. Viv Grigg was a single 28-year-old man when he first rented an upstairs room in a Manila slum from a hard-drinking, hard-gambling woman below. Early each morning he stood in line with neighbors at the nearby water spigot to get his bucket filled for the day (a chore that had to be completed before 6 a.m., when the city would cut off the flow in order to serve wealthier areas). When the women asked this tall, white-skinned man why he had chosen to live there, he answered, "I'm a follower of Jesus, who said He was called to preach good news to the poor."

The locals eyed him suspiciously at first, then gradually accepted his presence. In time they asked, "So when are you going to preach good news to us?" The door was now open for Grigg to set up a whiteboard in the open air and start telling the stories of the Bible. Eventually, more and more people stopped wasting what little money they had on alcohol and gambling, choosing rather to educate their children and build a more secure future. A full-fledged church took shape.

> Some Christian workers renounce their wealth and privilege to live among the poor. They swelter in the same heat, buy food in the same open-air markets, fight off the same rats, and try to sleep through the same sirens at night.

Years later, Grigg went on to do the same in tough sectors of Kolkata and Sao Paulo (where he met and married his Brazilian wife). He now teaches urban ministry at Azusa Pacific University in Los Angeles. Wherever he goes, he posits a three-step process for urban missionary work:

1. *Incarnation*—being the hands and feet of Jesus in the urban turbulence
2. *Proclamation*—verbalizing the message of Jesus, who was known for

such bold statements as "Blessed are the poor in spirit, for theirs is the kingdom of heaven" (Matthew 5:3). Says Grigg: "This is bigger than just proclaiming *salvation*. This is about *the kingdom*—God's reign in the world. What He wants to do is to change the whole order of things."

3. *Transformation*—seeing the gospel truth make real impact on individual lives and the larger society.

"The gospel moves among the poor ten times more rapidly than among the middle class," Grigg asserts. "Why? Because the Spirit seems more readily at work there. They are painfully aware of their lack in all areas of life, and they hope for some kind of help."

He points to John 12, where immediately after Jesus' teaching about the need for a kernel of wheat to fall into the ground and die, He adds, "Whoever serves me must follow me; and where I am, my servant also will be" (verse 26). If Jesus is at home in the slums, His people must be as well.

This kind of incarnational model has given birth to a global movement known as MoveIn. The effort was founded in 2009 by Nigel Paul, who lived in Toronto, Canada, amid a densely populated neighborhood of Pakistani and Afghan migrants. Since then, 25 new MoveIn teams have sprung up throughout Canada.

This mission philosophy is on full display at the annual "MoveIner Conference," where those who sense God's call to *move in* with the poor gather for teaching and information sharing. (See YouTube for multiple clips.)

More Than a Nice Gesture

In all of the above strategies, there is a temptation to stop short at meeting physical needs only. However, until the poor realize what lies behind the food, clothing, housing, education, and friendship coming their way, little is accomplished in Kingdom terms. Even Jesus said, in His comment about giving cups of cold water, that they should be given "in my name" (Mark 9:41). Without that, our service to a needy person or family is simply a nice humanitarian gesture.

As Viv Grigg puts it, after his decades of experience in some of the planet's worst environments, "The aim is not just incarnation. It's not even about planting a church. It is about transformation.

"You can be the nicest person in the world—but if you don't share the gospel, no one is going to come to Christ."[16]

Modern Christians in the West often like to quote St. Francis (1181-1226) as follows: "Preach the gospel at all times—and if necessary, use words." Their interpretation of this is that good deeds are often enough.

The only trouble is, scholars have never been able to find this sentence in the writings of St. Francis. The closest is an admonition to his friars that their lives should coincide with their preaching. He himself was an unceasing preacher, speaking as often as five times a day in the villages of Italy. According to his first biographer, Thomas of Celeno, "His words were neither hollow nor ridiculous, but filled with the power of the Holy Spirit, penetrating the marrow of the heart, so that listeners were turned to great amazement." (For a full treatment of this, see "Factchecker: Misquoting Francis of Assisi" at http://www.thegospelcoalition.org/article/factchecker-misquoting-francis of assisi.)

Actions are important. So are the motivations for those actions. Let us never deprive the poor—or anyone else—of "the gospel, because it is the power of God that brings salvation to everyone who believes" (Romans 1:16).

ASK YOURSELF

- *Have I actually seen the worst of my city's poverty? (If not, take a tour.)*
- *Who is already attempting to serve the poor in my area? Are these efforts being effective? If not, how could they be improved?*
- *What roles should I play that would be consistent with God's overall call for my life and ministry?*
- *In light of what I've read in this chapter, should my ministry priorities change in any way?*
- *How will I assist slum churches without dominating them, patronizing them, or breeding dependency?*

CHAPTER 7

Action 4: Reach Out to Diasporas

It is hard enough to manage today's urban lifestyle if you are native to the culture. The congestion, the mass transit system, the regulations of government, the social rules, the noise, and the rushed pace of life all present a sizable challenge to anyone.

How much more difficult it is for someone newly arrived from a much different place. The most basic things are foreign to them—where to find needed information, how to get medical care, how the school system works for the children, how even to sign up for phone or Internet service. And multiply every stress times two or three if the newcomer is having to function in a new language. Life can be overwhelming.

We use the word *diaspora* to describe these recently urbanized populations—a word that originally referred (capitalized) to Old Testament Jews exiled from Palestine and scattered across the nearby lands. Now the word (no capital) has been extended to mean "the movement, migration, or scattering of [any] people away from an established or ancestral homeland."[17] This certainly describes the reality in 21st-century cities, from Amsterdam to Accra to Atlanta to Adelaide.

The two charts on the next page show the 10 highest foreign-born percentages for populations across the world. The first shows the figures as a percent of all migrants (e.g., the United States is home to 20.2 percent of all the world's migrants), while the second shows the concentration within a given nation (e.g., 71.4 percent of everyone in the United Arab Emirates has come from somewhere else).

Country	Population in millions	% of all migrants	Major migrant communities of 20th and 21st Centuries
United States	38.4	20.2	European, African, Asian, Latin Am
Russia	12.1	6.4	Russian from former Soviet states
Germany	10.1	5.3	German from E Europe, Turks
France	6.4	3.4	North African, Black African
Saudi Arabia	6.4	3.3	Various
Canada	6.1	3.2	European, Asian, Latin American
India	5.7	3.0	South Asian, Tibetan
UK	5.4	2.8	Caribbean, South Asian, E European
Spain	4.7	2.2	North African, Latin American
Australia	4.1	2.2	European, Asian
Other countries	91.2	48.0	
World total	190.6	100.0	

Top 10 countries for foreign-born migrants (as a % of all migrants)

Country	Population in millions	% migrants	Major migrant communities of 20th and 21st Centuries
UAE	3.2	71.4	Global variety, Arab, Asian
Kuwait	1.7	62.1	Global variety, Arab, Asian
Singapore	1.8	42.6	Global variety, Asian, Caucasian
Israel	2.6	39.6	Returning Jews
Jordan	2.2	39.0	Arab, especially Palestinian
Saudi Arabia	6.4	25.9	Global variety, Arab, Asian
Oman	0.6	24.5	Global variety, Arab, Asian
Switzerland	1.6	22.9	European, Turks, Arabs
Australia	4.1	20.3	European, Asian, Middle Eastern
Canada	6.1	18.9	European, Asian, Hispanic

Top 10 countries for foreign-born migrants (as a % of the country's population)

Any ministry that aspires to reach a city for Christ must include diasporas in its vision. That is because whenever people migrate, they most often land in cities, not rural areas. They want to escape some kind of stress or danger where they are, or they want to find economic opportunity—and cities are the most logical hope for meeting these desires. (The one exception would be migrant farm workers, who come from another place to harvest crops. But these stay only for the growing season; they often don't bring their families with them, and once the work is done and they've collected their pay, they return home.)

Extending a Christian welcome to the immigrant is a predominantly urban challenge, and one of the most urgent challenges we face in urban ministry.

Move Quickly

The window of opportunity does not remain open indefinitely—no more than five years at the most. In the early days, newcomers are open to learn and make friendships as they get acquainted with their new environments. Their needs are immediate. The longer they stay, the more likely they are either to blend in with the indigenous population or to withdraw into ethnic ghetto communities that are closed to outsiders.

In some situations, Muslims have done better outreach than Christians. Abidjan, the capital of Cote d'Ivoire in West Africa, had very few indigenous Muslims in years past. But with turbulence rising across the region, many people have fled to the relatively stable economy of Abidjan—with the result that half the city's population today is Muslim. Granted, many were Muslim when they came, but many others became Muslim within six months of migrating to an urban center. Why? Because when they arrived homeless and without contacts in the city, they were invited to stay temporarily in the mosques until they could arrange more permanent housing. They naturally gravitated toward the religion that welcomed them.

Larry Holcomb, director of a New York City ministry called Urban Nations Outreach, says "Our biggest draw to get people to come to us are our free English classes. It's a serious need for these folks, and it's scary for them when they arrive; they're desperate to learn. As we demonstrate God's love in tangible ways, we gain the right to share the gospel."

Urban Nations Outreach also offers after-school programs for children, basic computer training, and citizenship classes. "There is an openness originally," Holcomb continues, "because they are in a new environment, and there's not as much social pressure as if they had taken an interest in the gospel in their own country.

"But it's a short window. After a while, they become integrated into their ethnic community, where they'll be advised not to listen to Americans, or to Christians. Many times I notice them becoming even stronger Muslims or Hindus here in the United States than they were back home."

In London, large groups of immigrants arrived from one small area in Bangladesh and another small area in Pakistan. Not feeling welcomed, they began organizing themselves in tight-knit communities that were very introspective, dedicating to preserving their culture and religion. Most of their imams were trained in Saudi Arabia, with all the consequences that entails. Wealthy South Asians began going to housing auctions, buying up large amounts of property to house these immigrants. Neighborhood mosques quickly sprang up. The result: London now has self-created ghettoes no more than a short Tube ride from Her Majesty's palace.

On the other hand, the government of Denmark has closely watched the ethnic concentrations taking shape in Copenhagen and has deliberately knocked down some high-rise apartment buildings in order to force Muslims to move out and assimilate more. Meanwhile, a Danish Christian leader named Hans-Henrik Lund has worked hard to bring together local churches, government agencies, and diaspora groups for dialogue. After pastoring City Church for 13 years, he is now the director of Church Integration Ministries, a specialty agency keyed to the needs of immigrants and internationals in Denmark. As a result, many different ethnic groups have been encouraged to start their own groups and congregations, often in partnership with indigenous churches.

Specialty Church or Blended Ones?

This brings us to a strategic question: How should urban and/or diaspora churches be formed and guided? Should a historic church with a heart for new immigrants seek to set up diaspora congregations, perhaps by hosting them in its building, or paying the rent for a stand-alone facility? Or should the ultimate aim be integration at every level?

Naturally, the first generation to arrive in a new place wants to hold onto their roots. They want to keep speaking the language of the homeland, share the same foods, and repeat the annual traditions and holidays. All of this argues in favor of ethnic-specific churches.

But their children and grandchildren—the second and third generations—badly want to assimilate to the new land. So does the "one-and-a-half generation"—those who were born elsewhere but were brought along as children. All of these want to learn English, or French, or whatever the prevailing language is, as quickly as possible—and without an accent! Their outlook is entirely aimed toward their future, not the past from which their forebears came.

Therefore, we must recognize that the stand-alone diaspora church is doomed after one-and-a-half to two generations. The young people simply won't stay around. This is being proven all over the world, whether by Korean-speaking churches in the United States or African-heritage churches across Europe.

On the other hand, if an ethnic group is welcomed into and accommodated by an established church, the younger generations have a place to move to. If an English-speaking church hosts a Chinese-speaking fellowship, the second generation can smoothly transition toward the English-speaking youth group—if they are made to feel welcome. The teenagers and children readily meld together.

Should a historic church with a heart for new immigrants seek to set up diaspora congregations by hosting them in its building, or should it rent a stand-alone facility? Should the ultimate aim be integration at every level?

This is not just "integration for integration's sake," to make an ideological point. There are practical benefits. Home-grown young people learn to understand and appreciate another culture. The immigrant young people find new friends, hopefully with positive moral values. Existing facilities are maximized, as opposed to going out and paying for new space.

And further down the road, this kind of experience often produces a higher number of recruits for missions. Huge numbers of Koreans and Chinese who migrated to the West have become earnest and effective missionaries. They're flexible, they're comfortable in multicultural settings, and they carry a heart for evangelism.

Eyes to See What God Sees

As established churches try to reach out to diaspora groups, there are likely to be occasional problems and misunderstandings along the way. Long-time members may question what's happening to "our church." They must grasp that, in fact, a church is not the private property of any human being or group; it is God's church. He cares for every person He created, regardless of their birthplace, mother tongue, passport registration—or lack thereof.

God made Himself perfectly clear to the "old-timers" of Israel: "When a foreigner resides among you in your land, do not mistreat them. The foreigner residing among you must be treated as your native-born. Love them as yourself, for you were foreigners in Egypt. I am the LORD your God" (Leviticus 19:33-34). Moses underscored this years later on God's behalf: "He defends the cause of the fatherless and the widow, and loves the foreigner residing among you, giving them food and clothing. And you are to love those who are foreigners, for you yourselves were foreigners in Egypt" (Deuteronomy 10:18-19). This remains our calling today.

Often, it may be less a case of actual mistreatment than it is simply not realizing or noticing the needs, and thus not responding. Tim Svoboda of YWAM writes with honesty about his work in Chennai (formerly Madras):

> For years in Chennai, which is the largest churched city of India, I kept my focus on the unreached beyond [i.e., missions at a distance]. However, I discovered that I was missing the unreached at my doorstep. Even though Chennai is predominately a monoethnic city [Tamil-speaking Hindus], it had large populations of unreached peoples that churches were not focusing on and did not want to focus on....
>
> Look carefully at your locations through proper research. It will unveil key segments of society that the Lord would lead us to engage.[18]

ASK YOURSELF

- *What is my personal attitude toward immigrants? (Be honest.)*
- *Where could I visit a diaspora church on a Sunday?*
- *While there, ask yourself: What needs do I see that I could address?*
- *Should I start a new effort to reach diasporas in my city?*

CHAPTER 8

Action 5: Form Healthy Churches

Bringing individual urban dwellers to the foot of the Cross—whether they be poor, rich, young, old, literate, illiterate, well-established, immigrant, or any other classification—is not the completion of our ministry task. Jesus has in mind for us to form these believers into something corporate that He called "church." While some other world religions may be basically solitary (Buddhism being one example), Christianity is "a group thing." It is designed to be lived out in regular community.

Formats around the world vary widely, of course. A video survey of urban churches in the 21st century would show everything from Yoido Full Gospel Church in downtown Seoul, South Korea (480,000 weekly attendance, using multiple sites, obviously)[19] to a circle of 30 or 40 people gathering under a tree in a park in Kinshasa, Democratic Republic of Congo; to a secret cell of Chinese believers praying quietly in a high-rise apartment.

Size is not the measure of a "healthy church." Neither is the presence or absence of a physical building. Some benefit from denominational affiliation, others are trying hard to reform and revive the denomination that claims them, and still others are quite independent.

In this chapter, we will focus on four of the characteristics of corporate Christianity in today's major cities.

A Healthy Urban Church is About Discipleship

A church that disciples engages in more than just singing and preaching. It goes deeper than simply putting on an enjoyable weekly event that draws an audience. The public meetings have their value, of course, but toward what purpose?

What Jesus actually said in the Great Commission is often misunderstood. The key words, at least in English, have been garbled. A careful study of the Greek text of Matthew 28:19 might result in this syntax (as one interlinear New Testament has it):

"Going therefore, disciple all the nations…."[20] The Master's emphasis was not on urging His followers to *go;* He assumed that would happen naturally. And neither did He tell them to "make disciples," as if it were some sort of manufacturing process in a factory. Instead, Jesus used the verb μαθητεύσατε, which translates somewhat awkwardly into English as "to disciple" or "to cause to become a follower." This is not so much a methodology as it is a lifestyle. If churches are not discipling people so that they become obedient to Jesus, they cannot claim to be fulfilling the Great Commission.

```
Those leaders who make discipling
their core work create replicas —
more intentional, dedicated
disciples of Christ.
```

But those leaders who make discipling their core work create replicas— more intentional, dedicated disciples of Christ. Every activity, every seminar, every sermon is geared toward bringing participants closer to the Jesus model. Some of this work may show up on the church schedule: for example, a class on Sunday morning or Tuesday night. Other aspects will be more organic. It may even be an online interaction that involves people's mobile phones.

An urban Nigerian pastor, Dr. Uzodinma Obed, resigned the church he had successfully founded (Glory Tabernacle in Ibadan) after 21 years in order to specialize in what he named the Apostolic Discipleship Movement (www. apostolicdiscipleshipmovement.org). Rather than stay in a comfortable pastorate, he turned the church over to a second generation of leaders so that he and his wife could give full time to developing discipleship materials for adults and also children, seeking to transform their Christian walk. The pair travels widely across their nation and beyond, raising awareness in churches and conferences of this critical need.

Discipleship is also more than curriculum. It includes learning to call upon God in prayer. Since I have already mentioned Ibadan (population 3 million), let me tell about preaching one Sunday in a different congregation there. The sanctuary was packed with some 400 people, almost all of them former Muslims. I finished my message, closed my Bible, turned, and sat down.

When I looked up again, the entire crowd had seemingly disappeared! Where had they gone so quickly? It took me a few seconds to realize that they were face-down on the floor, everyone praying as a response to the preaching of the Word.

Later, I asked the pastor, who was also a former Muslim, "Tell me about the spontaneous prayer time at the end of the sermon. Is this something that came from your Muslim background?"

"No, not at all," he replied. "It comes from Psalm 22:27, which says, 'All the ends of the earth will remember and turn to the Lord, and all the families of the nations will bow down before him.' And so that is what we do!"

I went away impressed anew with an urban church that was intent on following God with their whole heart.

A Healthy Urban Church Includes the Marginalized

As we noted in the previous chapter, cities are home to a wide variety of people, skills, languages, educational levels, and traditions. Healthy churches welcome this diversity, rather than trying to cloister themselves in homogeneous units. They stretch and accommodate, in obedience to the strong teaching of James chapter 2:

Suppose a man comes into your meeting wearing a gold ring and fine clothes, and a poor man in filthy old clothes also comes in. If you show special attention to the man wearing fine clothes and say, "Here's a good seat for you," but say to the poor man, "You stand there" or "Sit on the floor by my feet," have you not discriminated among yourselves and become judges with evil thoughts?

Listen, my dear brothers and sisters: Has not God chosen those who are poor in the eyes of the world to be rich in faith and to inherit the kingdom he promised those who love him? (verses 2-5)

When Ray Bakke and his wife went to pastor Chicago's Fairfield Avenue Baptist Church back in the late 1960s, they were concerned to avoid making their largely immigrant (Puerto Rican) congregation feel inferior. One day he came up with a novel idea:

I began by instructing the church secretary not to type the church bulletin "You are to teach other people how to type, so that they can get better jobs, and they can practice by doing the bulletin." [After that,] the bulletin sometimes went this way and sometimes that, and there were a few misspelled words, but it was the product of the members, and each issue bore the names of the women who had done the typing. Suddenly there was pride in the bulletin, and they were glad to give it out on Sundays.[21]

Another small gesture in the same congregation sent a big message to those whose life histories were somewhat checkered:

The only wealth of the poor are their children, and [so] our church directory noted all the children under their different surnames. Some families had six different names.[22]

This kind of inclusion, of meeting people where they are rather than wishing they had done better with their lives, evokes the spirit of Christ. He was entirely comfortable around the poor, the broken, the marginalized, those who were "other"—to the disapproval, we might add, of the religious establishment of his day. Pharisees and scribes criticized Him for His unsavory associations, but He was not deterred in the least.

Kensington Temple, based in the Notting Hill section of London, dates back to the 1930s and is the flagship church of the Elim Pentecostal movement. Its senior pastor, Colin Dye, is obviously English—although he was born in Kenya and also lived in Australia for a few years. Perhaps that has something to do with the fact that today's Kensington Temple is home to numerous cell groups that meet and worship in multiple languages, reflecting the diversity of this city. It is determined that its vision not be constrained just to the ethnic majority. Its motto says clearly, "London and the World for Christ."

A Healthy Urban Church May—or May Not—Have its Own Building

We are prone to forget that none of the New Testament churches we read about and so admire held actual property. Instead, they gathered "in the temple courts" (Acts 2:46) or "from house to house" (Acts 5:42); in Ephesus the apostle Paul "took the disciples with him and had discussions daily in the lecture hall of Tyrannus" (Acts 19:9).

Throughout the New Testament, the word *church* (ἐκκλησία in Greek) consistently signifies the "called-out ones" who follow Christ; it does not mean the roof over their heads. (A colloquialism in some parts of the American South is useful to preserve this distinction: the people are the "church," the building is the "church-house.")

> Inclusion—meeting people where they are rather than wishing they had done better with their lives— evokes the spirit of Christ.

This is not to say that church buildings are evil or counter to the divine intent, although they are unquestionably expensive to build and then to maintain. In many cultures today, they are considered mandatory if a congregation wants to gain any respect among the general public.

However, in a number of urban environments, where property and construction is so very costly, some churches have elected not to invest in buildings. Instead, they rent space from others. When Mark Batterson and a few others started National Community Church in Washington, D.C. in 1996, they deliberately chose to anchor their meetings in a cinema theater inside the historic Union (train) Station less than 15 minutes' walk from the United States Capitol.

Their outreach, especially to government workers, has enlarged today to ten weekly services that meet in seven different locations across the city— all in movie palaces. In fact, they are known for their website address, www. theaterchurch.com. More than once, Batterson has joked that the promotional tag line for their advertising should be "Coming Soon to a Theater Near You!"

National Community Church finally did buy a piece of Washington real estate a few years back—an abandoned diner (again, on Capitol Hill) that it turned into a bustling coffeehouse called Ebenezer's. Small groups, Bible studies, and informal conversations about Christ take place here seven days a week. This illustrates the church's manifesto, which begins as follows:

We are ...
more afraid of missing opportunities than making mistakes. We are a lab where everything is an experiment. If the Kingdom of God had departments, we'd be R&D. There are ways of doing church that no one has thought of yet. We are orthodox in belief, but unorthodox in practice.

We believe ...
that if you want to reach people no one is reaching, you have to do things no one is doing. A church that stays within its four walls isn't a church at all. We don't go to church because we ARE the church.

Some urban churches, having worked long and hard to build impressive buildings, have then had them taken away by hostile governments and been forced to endure without them. The most startling examples are in China, where some congregations, though duly registered as part of the government-approved Three-Self Patriotic Movement, have watched in tears when bulldozers arrived to knock down their sanctuaries. The accusation in the spectacular case of Sanjiang Church in Wenzhou was that the eight-story building that took six years to build (drawing previous praise as a "model project") was too large for zoning codes; its bright red cross on top may have been particularly galling to local authorities.[23]

Such a blow, however, will do nothing to quench Christian vitality in the cities of China. The church of Jesus Christ will go on, building or no building.

A Healthy Urban Church Finds Ways around Obstacles

One of the reasons Nigerian church planters seem to do well, I believe, is that they have grown adept at side-stepping problems and difficulties that would daunt others. They learned this on their home soil, and now they are doing the same on other continents. Sunday Adelaja's remarkable work in Ukraine is just one example. The Kiev church has some 25,000 members, and another 600 daughter/satellite congregations have been planted across 45 nations.

But they are not the only ones. In cities across the Muslim world, God seems to be giving special creativity to those who carry His light. Iran, for example, is seeing massive church growth, and the courage of those Christians is astounding. Elam Ministries (www.elam.com) started a Bible translation project in the Farsi language. When the New Testament went to press, a million copies were printed. Moving on to work on the Old Testament, one translator was asked to be the team leader—only to be arrested by the ayatollahs and killed.

I saw a video clip of a government cabinet minister holding up a copy of the New Testament on TV and saying, "Look at this thing the Christians have produced—it's beautiful! But don't buy it!" Of course, that was the best advertising that Elam could hope for. Iranian young people seem to delight in doing exactly opposite of what the government advises.

It is not unreasonable to say now that there are more than 500,000 believers in Iran. They meet in house groups far and wide, with no more than 12 members each. They use special mechanisms: Rather than announcing their meetings in advance, they decide on the location at the last minute. Then someone goes and stands at a certain intersection, where believers stop by to get the actual address for the night.

One estimate says that 60 to 70 percent of all Iranians are watching

Christian television. At one point, the government banned all satellite dishes. But certain cabinet ministers became so rich selling illegal dishes that the corruption defeated the ideology.

In a slightly less restricted country such as Turkey, which is still 97 percent Muslim, the Istanbul Protestant Church has formed a "foundation" that the government recognizes as legitimate. Four active congregations are members of the foundation—two in Istanbul, and two others outside the city.

An art director from Spain, Carlos Madrigal, moved there with his family back in 1985 to learn the Turkish language and to work in various advertising agencies while he completed theological training. Since then, he has managed to convince government authorities that Christianity has a long and honorable history in this land, citing the first-century churches of Ephesus, Colossae, Troas, Smyrna, and others. Therefore, he said, it should not be considered "foreign" for Christian bodies to exist in Turkey today, as long as they abide by current laws. His winsome manner has prevailed. (See www.istpcf.org for more information.)

These are but some of the markers of healthy urban churches in the 21st century. No doubt others could be enumerated as well. All of them remind us that, when Jesus said, "I will build my church, and the gates of Hades will not overcome it" (Matthew 16:18), He made no exceptions for difficult environments. His vision for the church was truly worldwide.

Today, in cities across the globe, from east to west, from north to south, that vision is moving steadily forward.

ASK YOURSELF

- As a congregation gets larger, how can the main task of discipling remain central, despite the demands of large-group worship with all its organization and choreography?
- What is the most biblical leadership model? Or have I unconsciously taken my cues from Western corporate and commercial hierarchies instead? What is the main point of leadership anyway—"to equip [Christ's] people for works of service" (Ephesians 4:12), or to control a burgeoning organization?
- How do marginalized groups and subgroups feel about our church? Do they sense a welcome, or are they viewed as a hindrance to our overall "image"?
- In our spending, how important has investing in buildings and furnishings become compared to investing in outreach (both local and cross-cultural)?
- Finally, a general question: What elements, traditions, or values are limiting us (even unintentionally) from being an effective and biblical church? What might I do about that?

CHAPTER 9

Action 6:
Confront Sinful Structures

Dr. Viv Grigg remembers a conversation with two young men on a sidewalk next to a Bangkok slum. "Tell me about this area," he innocently inquired. "What is life like here?"

"Well," came the reply, "the whole place gets burned down every seven years. Everybody loses all their belongings and has to start over."

Grigg obviously was taken aback and asked why.

The two explained that a Thai law says that if someone squats on a piece of land for seven years, they gain certain rights to stay there. Therefore, the landowner makes sure that before the seven-year mark comes around, a mysterious fire drives out all squatters. If some people lose their lives in the chaos, well ...

We could wish that such an outrage were the rare exception across our planet, but it is not. The apostle John was not exaggerating when he wrote, "We know ... that the whole world is under the control of the evil one" (1 John 5:19). Selfishness, greed, treachery, and exploitation are so ingrained in the human heart that they have long ago become institutionalized in the laws and customs of nations. And not just primitive or pagan nations; the "enlightened" countries of the "Christian West" are guilty as well.

And nowhere is this more true than in major cities.

While many Christians have turned fatalistic and assumed nothing could be changed until the perfect city, the New Jerusalem, is installed, others have worked bravely and tirelessly to change sinful structures. More than one has used the analogy of a swiftly flowing river with frantic bodies tumbling downstream, hitting boulders as they go. Yes, we should pull these poor souls out of the water and wrap them in warm blankets, it is said. But should we not also find out who is pushing them into the river up above, and stop the carnage at its source?

> While many Christians await the perfect city, the New Jerusalem, others have worked bravely and tirelessly to change sinful structures in the cities of our world.

It is Not Enough to Bemoan

Ray Bakke points to the Old Testament drama of Esther and says, "The message of this book is that when sin gets written into the law code, you can't just repudiate it. You've got to access power and change it....

"Some people have to go inside the black holes of politics and practice power and change law. This is absolutely true. You can't just change the streets on the streets. People have to go up to power and down to the powerless."[24]

One example of this change is what Thomas Hieber has been accomplishing in the German capital of Berlin. As everyone knows, this city suffered a traumatic division all throughout the Cold War. When the infamous Berlin Wall was torn down in 1989, the city was reunited, but many challenges and inequalities remained. The ethnic composition of the 4.5 million residents was a huge challenge. Some 30 percent were born in another country, and probably around 40 percent are not indigenous German.

Thomas Heiber has been used of God to bring together a wide range of churches and organizations to make a difference in Berlin. The network that emerged was entitled Gemeinsam für Berlin (GfB), or "Together for Berlin." Regular meetings for sharing ideas and strategies to impact the city were instituted, and significant changes resulted in cleaning up graffiti and rubbish, addressing social and economic pains, bringing together different ethnic networks—all with a gospel center. This dynamic, flexible network, composed of those who normally would not have met together, has been transformational for the city. (See www.gfberlin.de for more information.)

In Europe or, to a lesser degree, North America, secularists sometimes make it very tough for Christians to work on public issues. They will accuse believers of ulterior motives, of "pushing religion into the public square." They will even twist good proposals, maligning them as "bigoted" or "insensitive."

But the cause of justice is too important to concede. God's love for all humanity must have advocates to demonstrate its supreme worth.

Battling Powers and Principalities

A multinational force to be reckoned with is the International Justice Mission, which works in some twenty major cities[25] on three continents. The IJM targets six modern evils:

- Slavery
- Sex trafficking (forced prostitution, often using children and teens as well as adults)
- Sexual violence (molestation, rape)
- Police brutality
- Property grabbing (taking land and buildings from those to whom it rightfully belongs)
- Citizens' rights abuse (e.g., withholding official identification, which makes getting a job or defending yourself against accusations nearly impossible).

The IJM model is to bring lawyers and social workers alongside of local law enforcement officials who care about the abuses going on but are often overwhelmed with trying to turn the tide. These lawyers also help draft needed legislation and then lobby for its passage. "We don't stop at rescuing people after they have been abused," says the IJM website (www.ijm.org). "Our ultimate goal is to prevent the violence from happening in the first place."

As mentioned earlier, this kind of intervention by Christians is needed in more than just the red-light districts of Mombasa or the brick kilns of India. The American city of Portland, Oregon—despite its leafy parks, art exhibits, bike-friendly trails, and "City of Roses" image—has been embarrassed in recent years to be singled out as the nation's "epicenter of child prostitution."[26] For every coffee shop and independent bookstore in the city, there is a dimly lit backroom where children are sold for sex. Two-thirds of all schools are within a mile of a strip club.

But local Christians, with IJM encouragement, have been rising up to fight this tawdry wickedness. They formed an action group called the Oregon Center for Christian Voices (OCCV) and began working with the local police department to crack down on sexual exploitation. Says OCCV's leader, Mr. Shoshon Tama-Sweet, "When you have this evil—people who enslave another human being's body and turn it into something sexually exploited on a daily basis for financial gain—this is the antithesis of what God wants. This is the antithesis of a beloved community."

Girls have been rescued out of the sex trade, pimps have been arrested and sent to jail, the state legislature has been persuaded to raise the fine for purchasing sex from a minor from $800 to $10,000. Another bill has removed the "age defense" in court (when a defendant claims, "But she said she was 18 years old," even though the frightened girl was no doubt younger).

An activist named Esther Nelson managed to get one of the pastors at her church onto the city government's special committee on child exploitation. He says, "People of salt and light [should be] infiltrating every one of these institutions. We want to be part of the solution, as opposed to coming only if we are leading the discussion."

One of the committee members who works for Multnomah County (Portland's jurisdiction) extends an open invitation. "The church in the best position to take the lead on morality issues in a way that government can't," says Joslyn Baker. "At the end of the day, we put the bad guy away and get [the girl] clothes and health treatment. But who loves her? Who tells her a story other than 'The only thing you're good for is selling your body'?"

Reinforcement for her viewpoint comes from the OCCV leader. "The church has something special: We have the good news. We have a vision of the way the world is supposed to be. And it doesn't include the rape of children on our streets.

"When you realize that God loved every victim when they were born, that He's with them every day they're traumatized—it's incumbent upon believers to protect them, to help them become whole."[27]

Pushing back against the evil forces of this world's urban societies is not pleasant work. But the realities of our cities demand it. Jesus did not observe the greedy temple merchants who were price-gouging the poor and simply shake His head. He picked up a rope and did something about it.

We must follow His example.

ASK YOURSELF

- *In my particular city, how is the law or the power structure weighted against righteousness?*
- *What attempts, if any, have been made so far to rectify these injustices?*
- *What still needs to be done?*
- *Who could join me in this struggle? Where might I find allies?*

CHAPTER 10

Action 7:
Address Real Human Pain Directly

None of what was said in the previous chapter should be used to eclipse our direct response to the daily pain of those in today's cities. The hungry, the ill, the addicted, the mentally tormented, the homeless, the school-less, the coat-less, the alone-and-pregnant—all of these are suffering on a personal level and need our prompt response. Yes, there ought to be systemic programs to address these matters over the long term, and we can work toward creating them. But in the meantime, the individual in distress must be helped.

The church has been doing this for centuries, and now is no time to quit just because it seems passé. When we read Jesus' story about the man who was robbed on the road down to Jericho, we hear nothing about the need for better police protection on that stretch of highway, or faster ambulance service. We only see an ordinary man (a Samaritan, no less) stopping to help the bruised and battered victim. His action was not particularly convenient; it cost the Samaritan extra time and money. Yet Jesus said to His nervous hearers that day, "Go and do likewise" (Luke 10:37).

Christians, in fact, have an advantage in these things by virtue of the fact that they can move more efficiently than others, if they have the will to do so. They don't have to ask government bureaucracies for permits or grants of money. They don't have to write thick policy manuals or mount expensive media campaigns. They don't even really need to debate with each other about the theology of such action.

The apostle Paul writes in Galatians 2 about his confrontation with the apostle Peter over Gentile status in the Body of Christ. He cites the opinion of the Jerusalem council (see Acts 15) to bolster his viewpoint. But at the end of the passage, Paul adds, almost as a footnote, "All they [the pillars of the Jerusalem leadership] asked was that we should continue to remember the poor, the very thing I had been eager to do all along" (Galatians 2:10).

It is as if he is implying, *We may have our differences about Gentiles in the church; we may not see eye to eye on the topic of circumcision—but at least we don't need to argue about helping those in need! That should be obvious to all parties.*

> Christians and their churches often have an advantage in serving the poor. They can move efficiently, if they want to. They don't have to ask government bureaucracies for permits or grants of money. They don't have to write thick policy manuals or mount expensive media campaigns.

Fueled by Love

Differing needs call for differing responses, of course. Setting up to feed 300 children a day is not at all the same as sheltering a teenage mother-to-be or guiding a heroin addict toward freedom. Most urban churches and ministries do not attempt to cope with all the hurts around them. As St. Francis de Sales put it 500 years ago, "It is far better to do a few things well than to undertake many good works and leave them half done."

But as St. Paul tells us, in all cases, "Christ's love compels us, because we are convinced that … he died for all, that those who live should no longer live for themselves but for him who died for them and was raised again." Paul goes on a few verses later to declare something that should echo in the heart of every Kingdom worker: "We are therefore Christ's ambassadors, as though God were making his appeal through us. We implore you on Christ's behalf: Be reconciled to God" (2 Corinthians 5:14-15, 20).

This central message is embedded deeply into the work, for example, of Betel International, an intensive mission to drug and alcohol addicts that started in a Madrid barrio in 1985 and has since replicated itself in more than 100 other cities across 24 nations. Named for the "house of God" (Genesis 28:17) that Jacob discovered in his hour of loneliness, Betel (in Spanish; "Bethel" in English) invites the addicted to come and live in a community of love and faith for 12 to 18 months, and to discover new life in Christ. A disciplined schedule, morning devotional times as a group, one-to-one counseling, plus being assigned to one of Betel's work teams set a whole new pattern for those who have floundered in self-destruction.

A Welshman, former addict, and Betel resident named Steve says:

Everything in my life took a turn for the worse when I was 11 years old. My father left home, and soon after I began experimenting with alcohol and sniffing solvents. Five years later I moved on to cannabis, ecstasy, and speed. I was never really addicted to any substance until the moment I took heroin. It hooked me straight away.

My addiction got to the point where I couldn't even eat without a 'hit.' Eventually, there was no more 'high.' I had to take the drug just to function. I overdosed eight times, and was in and out of jail for six years. During my last stint in prison, I decided that I wanted to change, but I didn't know how. I couldn't break free of my addiction.

Another eight years passed before some Christian friends told me that Jesus could heal me. I began to pray, but I'd been an addict so long, I didn't know how to change my behaviour. One day, a friend found out about Betel on the Internet, and I decided to give it a go. The moment I entered the doors, I felt at peace and at home. Although it was difficult at first, I soon began to live a different way—I found I could get out of bed and eat without taking drugs!

Today, I live in the knowledge that God has set me free, from both my addictions and my old ways of thinking. As the Bible promises, I've been changed ... my mind's been renewed.

The Betel program accepts both men and women. "Some 50 to 60 percent of people are homeless when they come to us; 70 percent have multiple criminal convictions," says Kent Martin, director of the Birmingham (U.K.) facility. Yet Martin has never had to call the police for intervention, demonstrating the power of the gospel to set free from drugs and crime.

A unique aspect is Betel's financial structure. It charges no fees to anyone, and it accepts no government aid. Instead, up to 90 percent of its operating costs are earned from businesses that the work teams operate—everything from furniture restoration to gardening/landscaping services to chicken farms. In this way, skills are taught for the future, and profits are gleaned in the present. Donations and trust funds, meanwhile, must supply the other 10 percent.

Furthermore, anyone entering a Betel program is required to sign off from all public benefits (welfare payments) that he or she may be receiving. "That changes everything," says Martin. "People immediately have to face up to taking personal responsibility."

The courts and police are uniformly positive about Betel's results, even if they don't fully understand what makes it succeed. Centers are now operating from Mexico to Kazakhstan, from Australia to Germany, with 3,000 participants receiving help at any given time. After conducting an observation, one Birmingham Mail reporter wrote, "I've never met so many troubled souls under one roof in a single day—and then left feeling so positive about the world at large."[28] (For more information, see: www.betelinternational.org.)

This kind of ministry obviously feeds fresh life into nearby churches, and in some cases has led to the planting of new churches altogether. While the Madrid treatment center currently houses some 200 people who are recovering from addictions, the nearby Betel church welcomes 600 worshipers on Sunday.

The Key to Lasting Social Change

This kind of change—from the inside out—is key for any ministry dealing with the distressed. External adjustments will only go so far and will often fade away over time. I remember traveling along the Senegal River valley in West Africa, which is a terribly hot place with dust everywhere. All along the river, I saw abandoned aid projects. Some good had been done in those places, but as soon as the foreigners (and their money) left, it had all gone back to the desert.

Social change without heart change doesn't work. What is the use of filling someone's stomach, or clothing their body, if they end up in a lost eternity? The commission of Jesus was to *disciple* them, remember? In our attention to physical needs, we must never neglect the good news that redeems the troubled, sinful soul.

> In our attention to meeting physical needs, we must never neglect the good news that redeems the troubled, sinful soul.

We must also speak the truth if we see that unhealthy dependency is starting to settle in. The Scripture speaks clearly in calling men and women toward self-sufficiency over time. It warns those who "are idle and disruptive ... to settle down and earn the food they eat." Yet the very next verse says to the rest of us, "And as for you, brothers and sisters, never tire of doing what is good" (2 Thessalonians 3:11-13).

It is sometimes hard to strike the right balance between charity and a call to personal responsibility. Certainly we must help the young, the disabled, and the elderly for longer periods than those who are capable of maintaining themselves in life. God will give wisdom in each case so that we discern the best ways to proceed.

Working Together

One organization that has given much thought to this question—and to the best efficiencies as well—is Love INC. (The "INC" stands not for "Incorporated" but rather as an acronym for "... In the Name of Christ.") Born in the 1970s in the U.S.A., it is now being implemented in Kenya as well. Its origins go back to two dysfunctions: (1) church members having almost no avenue to help the poor and marginalized directly, assuming that special agencies (the Salvation Army, the rescue missions, or certainly the government) would take care of that; and (2) scheming indigents who go from one church to another asking for multiple handouts.

A man named Virgil Gulker asked himself why the churches in a given community couldn't coordinate their benevolence giving through a clearinghouse, and in the process get church people from all across the city involved with actual hands-on service. If a single mother could not afford winter clothing and shoes for her children, let a trained advocate come alongside her and find the right items in the right sizes from any number of donors in any number of churches. And beyond that? Start providing instruction and contacts for the single mom to get onto a more sure financial footing, so that future pleas for help could be minimized.

In his book *Help Is Just Around the Corner,* Gulker told about one man named Don:

> He presented himself as an ex-convict, and he was. But from that point he left facts behind and roamed in the realm of fiction. His standard story was that because of his criminal record, no one would hire him. He claimed also to have a physical ailment, which varied between a stomach disorder to a foot problem, depending on the situation. He would go to pastors, claiming to be in town for the first time. However, he refused to stay in a mission shelter and insisted on being put up at a particular motel.
>
> I have since discovered a fair amount about Don. I can go into any community in my home area of Michigan and describe Don's *modus operandi* without mentioning his name, and both agency folks and pastors will immediately say, "You mean Don!" ... He always carries sufficient cash to prevent being arrested for vagrancy, and he maintains a post office box in one Michigan town where he receives disability checks from Social Security.[29]

To prevent this kind of chicanery, Love INC (www.loveinc.org) was created. It began tracking who was asking for what, how much assistance was given, and by which churches or agencies. Christians of good will began to feel more confident that their help was actually going to benefit the needy. Churches— large ones, small ones, liberal ones, conservative ones—started finding ways to work together in lifting up the name of Christ among the distressed.

Today, 100,000 Love INC volunteers from 8,600 churches are making a difference in 157 cities and regions. The most recent tally showed 1,680,000 individual needs being addressed in a year's time.

The benefits of Christian cooperation in meeting human needs are sizable. Often an outside voice—an expatriate missionary, for example—can bring together Christian groups that have never really spoken to each other, focusing their attention on the crying needs at hand. New bridges of help can be built. Whatever the organizing process, the results in touching real human needs are invaluable.

What about Us?

Meanwhile, we have not even yet spoken about what ministry to those in distress does to *us,* the helping population. It stretches our compassion. It opens our eyes to the daily realities of the have-nots. It shows us that, by comparison, our own problems are hardly worth complaining about. It guides us to take seriously the word that says, "If anyone has material possessions and sees a brother or sister in need but has no pity on them, how can the love of God be in that person? Dear children, let us not love with words or speech but with actions and in truth" (1 John 3:17-18).

It also sends a powerful message to our children and others who are watching us. It breaks into their self-centeredness and obsession with material goods. Tim Svoboda, the YWAM leader quoted earlier, has written about the importance of location in training young recruits for ministry. Rather than sheltering them on safe academic-style campuses in the countryside, he says:

> I am finding around the world that students in our DTS's [Discipleship
> Training Schools] and other training programs are excited when they are
> being taught in locations that have hell in their front yards. In once such
> base that I know, you literally walk out their front door and are slapped

in the face by drug addicts, derelicts, homeless and the lost. The DTS students have to struggle with not only facing their own problems but are interacting each day with those outside their door who are in much worse conditions than themselves.[30]

We may draw inspiration from the example of the scion of a wealthy English family in the late 1800s named C. T. Studd. Educated in the best schools (Eton and Cambridge), he was a star cricketer, playing on the national team in 1882. Yet when God called him to missionary work, he gave away his inherited fortune and spent the rest of his life among the needy, first in China, then in South India, until his health broke. Once he recovered, he sailed for Africa this time (against his doctors' advice), where he founded the Heart of Africa Mission. He eventually died in the Congo at age 70 and is buried there. Meanwhile, his mission had expanded to become the Worldwide Evangelization Crusade (WEC), with which my wife and I have served for many years.

Perhaps C. T. Studd's best known epigram is this one, which motivates and challenges us to this day. It is especially relevant to the needs of the suffering in 21st-century cities:

Some wish to live within the sound of church or chapel bell;
I want to run a rescue shop within a yard of hell.

ASK YOURSELF

- *If my city had a "misery index," who would be suffering the worst?*
- *To which of these groups might God be calling me?*
- *What might I attempt to do first? Second? Third?*
- *How will I integrate the gospel into my social efforts?*

CHAPTER 11

Action 8: Embrace a Wider Vision

Our final critical response to the urban challenge is for city churches to embrace a vision for spreading the gospel beyond their own sectors. This may seem unreasonable to expect. We can well imagine the urban pastor saying, "My goodness, I can hardly deal with the needs of my own neighborhood. We have crime on every hand, drugs being sold in open view, schools that are overcrowded and deteriorating, families falling apart, the homeless sleeping in alleys … and you want to talk to me about faraway *missions?*"

Yet the Great Commission mandate bears no exclusion clauses for hardship. We find in the words of Jesus no "except for …" language. His final statement before ascending back to His Father (Acts 1:8) promised us the power of the Spirit in order to be His witnesses in a set of concentric circles: first, our home city ("Jerusalem"), next our home region ("Judea"), then our neighboring region ("Samaria"), and finally "to the ends of the earth."

It is a curiosity that in our time, many urban congregations speak of their mission field only in local terms, making this the sole focus of their mission work. It has led to a redefining of "mission" to include almost anything done for local non-members, but in doing so, the Great Commission has been parochialized.

Any church without a full-orbed Acts 1:8 vision is no longer a biblical church.

First-Century Examples

We have already mentioned in a previous chapter that the Antioch church readily commissioned missionary teams to head out to the hinterlands of Asia Minor. "After they had fasted and prayed, they placed their hands on them and sent them off" (Acts 13:3). These teams came back periodically to report on their work (see Acts 14:26-27; also 18:22-23), then headed out again.

Younger, more fledgling churches as well stepped up to meet needs in far-off places. These congregations were not particularly rich. No doubt they faced local needs of their own. Still, Paul reports concerning the believers of Philippi, Thessalonica, and Berea:

> And now, brothers and sisters, we want you to know about the grace that God has given the Macedonian churches. In the midst of a very severe trial, their overflowing joy **and their extreme poverty** welled up in rich generosity. For I testify that they gave as much as they were able, and even beyond their ability. Entirely on their own, they urgently pleaded with us for the privilege of sharing in this service to the Lord's people. And they exceeded our expectations (2 Corinthians 8:1-5, emphasis added).

Paul then challenges his readers in Corinth to do at least as much.

More than once we read of gospel workers laboring far from their home base. Timothy, a native of Lystra, was deployed to Ephesus (see 1 Timothy 1:3) and later requested to come to Rome (2 Timothy 4:11). Epaphroditus, from Philippi, is shown to be in Rome helping the imprisoned apostle—and getting seriously sick in the process (Philippians 2:25-30). Tychicus, apparently from Ephesus, was sent to Colossae (Colossians 4:7-9). If we had a "passport" for Titus, it would show him all over the eastern Mediterranean: Jerusalem (Galatians 2:1), Macedonia (2 Corinthians 7:5-7), Corinth at least twice (2 Corinthians 7:7 and 8:16-17), even the remote island of Crete for an extended season (Titus 1:5). None of these men "stayed home" to limit their attention to ministry needs at hand. They carried God's burden for the larger world.

Examples Today

Turning to our own century, we see any number of urban churches reaching out beyond their city limits—and growing stronger for their efforts. South Korean missionaries are found everywhere, it seems; their nation is now said to have sent the second largest contingent of Kingdom workers outside their home country.

Their neighbors next door in China are also making a sizable impact, despite governmental restrictions. As the Christian community across China has become more urban (especially since the Tiananmen Square upheaval of 1989), more finances have become available, with the result that Chinese missionaries are appearing far and wide. The Chinese church has even birthed a grand "Back to Jerusalem" vision, believing that God has called them to play a strategic role in fulfilling the Great Commission, working from east to west. (See www.backtojerusalem.com.)

Africa is stepping up as well. Once again, the limitation of finances is not being allowed to squelch the missionary vision. In a *Mission Frontiers* article, Bruce Koch reports on what is happening continent-wide—and beyond:

> Because of the dominance of Christianity in the southern half of Africa, the catchphrase for casting vision is not surprisingly "Go North!" The challenge Sub-Saharan Africans see when they look to the North is not only the Arab countries of North Africa; *they see beyond the Mediterranean to a post-Christian Europe* (italics added).
>
> Both of these contexts are quite different culturally from the "heart of Africa." If Africans are going to be effective in evangelism and church planting as they send to the North, they will certainly have to learn how to do things differently from the methods they have used closer to home. But if the most important ingredient in opening the eyes of the lost is seeing the faith lived out in good soil of lives filled with His Spirit, Africa has a lot to offer.[31]

As just one example of African initiative, consider the Redeemed Christian Church of God denomination (www.trccg.org/rccg). From its headquarters in Lagos, Nigeria, and its base of some 2,000 congregations across that country, it has planted churches in 178 other nations, including England, Germany,

France, the United States, Canada, Australia, the Philippines, India, Pakistan, and even the United Arab Emirates.

Its Mission and Vision statement minces no words. It lists the following objectives:

1. To make heaven.

2. To take as many people with us as possible.

3. To have a member of RCCG in every family of all nations.

To accomplish No. 1 above, holiness will be our lifestyle.

To accomplish No. 2 and 3 above, we will plant churches within five minutes walking distance in every city and town of developing countries, and within five minutes driving distance in every city and town of developed countries.

We will pursue these objectives until every nation in the world is reached for the Lord Jesus Christ.

No wonder a *New York Times* writer called the RCCG "one of [Africa's] most vigorously expansionary religious movements, a homegrown Pentecostal denomination that is crusading to become a global faith."[32] Whatever one may think of its style or doctrinal specifics, there is no denying that the group is serious about the Great Commission.

Waiting Fields

This kind of larger vision does not drain an urban church; it energizes it. People sense that they are part of something global. They hear Jesus saying to His small-minded disciples concerned about getting lunch, "I tell you, open your eyes and look at the fields! They are ripe for harvest. Even now the one who reaps draws a wage and harvests a crop for eternal life, so that the sower and the reaper may be glad together" (John 4:35-36).

Every individual pastor and church must frame its own action plan, of course. Priorities must be set, in accordance with the well-known outline of "Pray-Give-Go." (Some churches add a fourth item, so that it reads, "Pray-Learn-Give-Go.") All of us can certainly pray for the evangelization of the world. All of us can spend time learning about mission endeavors. Nearly all of us can give funds to advance the gospel. And in this day when travel is easier than ever before, many of us can go—if not long-term, then short-term.

We must give our attention to the things that move the heart of God. Why? Because across the teeming cities of our world today, it is harvest time.

ASK YOURSELF

- *What am I and my fellow believers doing now that reaches outside the boundaries of our city? What is my congregation's vision for this?*
- *What might God be asking me to consider for the future?*
- *How might I organize that? What shape would such an involvement take?*
- *Who would I have to convince to participate with us?*

CHAPTER 12

Conclusion:
Greater Things are Still to Come

In this book, we have taken a clear-eyed look at the rising tide of urbanization. We have faced the reality that the world is already more than 50 percent urban, and is headed for 90 percent by the end of this century. We have confronted our own prejudices and assumptions about city life. We have also sought to know what God thinks and feels about cities.

It would be foolish, of course, to sit and do nothing in the face of urban facts. Though we might feel initially overwhelmed, as I was that first day in a Johannesburg shantytown looking out the car window at the squalor and hopelessness, we have gathered up our courage and begun to explore eight vital responses:

1. Praying together for God to show mercy on cities and spread His light through us

2. Exegeting the particular city to which we are called, so that we know more about what and who it actually contains

3. Pushing strongly against urban poverty, refusing to accept the status quo of the suffering

4. Reaching out to new arrivals in the city—the immigrant communities often ignored

5. Forming healthy churches to welcome and disciple believers in their Christian walk
6. Tackling the institutional structures that oppress and demean ordinary citizens
7. Meeting real human bondages and shortages on a personal level
8. Looking above our immediate circumstances to the wider work of God across the world

What Next?

In each case, we have given examples of these responses—certainly not an exhaustive catalog by any means, but enough to stimulate our imaginations. No doubt the reader has, in the process, remembered other, even better, strategies—or has begun to dream about what could be birthed.

Though urbanization is a huge, complex phenomenon, we can press ahead "through him who gives [us] strength" (Philippians 4:13). This is no time for surrender. We are doing what Jesus said for us to do! We focus not on the difficulties but on the steps God would have us take on His behalf. He is already at work in the modern megacities; we are His willing workforces.

A contemporary Christian band from Northern Ireland named Bluetree was on a mission trip to Thailand a few years back. They went to play their music in the city of Pattaya (area population 1 million) some 100 kilometers southeast of Bangkok. This beachfront metropolis is the epicenter of Thailand's sun-sand-and-sex-for-purchase industry. Everywhere the band looked, they saw tourists coming to buy personal pleasure in the go-go bars, massage parlors, and hourly-rate hotels. They could not miss colorful advertising for cabaret shows where transsexual and transgender entertainers perform to packed houses. Understandably, pickpockets eyed the tourists on every sidewalk.

Rather than pulling back in revulsion, Aaron Boyd and his fellow musicians were stirred with God's passion for Pattaya. What might God want to accomplish in this modern version of Sodom? A song began to be born. The melody line began in a soft, low range:

> *You're the God of this City*
> *You're the King of these people*
> *You're the Lord of this nation*
> *You are*

You're the Light in this darkness
You're the Hope to the hopeless
You're the Peace to the restless
You are

Next came a musical "bridge," building in intensity....

There is no one like our God
There is no one like our God

Finally, in full-throated declaration, came the chorus:

For greater things have yet to come
And greater things are still to be done in this city
Greater things have yet to come
And greater things are still to be done in this city[33]

It was Bluetree's battle cry for the triumph of the Kingdom of God over the powers of darkness and sin.

The band began performing the song in concerts back home. They recorded it in 2007. Audiences rose to its courageous vision. Then one night as they were "opening" (performing the initial set) for a Chris Tomlin concert in Belfast, they sang the song. One of Tomlin's associates heard it and was struck. He quickly went backstage to his friend and said, "Did you hear that song they just did? It's amazing."

Tomlin had not. But once he did, he too was captured by its driving passion. He sought permission to record it himself. Since then, "God of This City" has swept around the world, being sung in churches, and winning "Song of the Year 2009" in the Worship Leader Magazine Readers' Choice Awards. (To watch a nine-minute video in which Chris Tomlin tells the story of discovering the song and then performs it for the interviewer, go to: http://worshiptogether.com/songs/songdetail.aspx?iid=979895.)

Greater things ... greater progress ... greater light ... greater redemption for those in the grip of urban despair and confusion. This is God's will for the 21st century. And we get the high privilege of helping Him make it happen.

Notes

1 Pew Research Global Attitudes Project, "Deepening Economic Doubts in India," Sept. 10, 2012, chap. 4.

2 As reported in *Science* magazine, "World population stabilization unlikely this century," Oct. 10, 2014.

3 http://www.ywamsanfrancisco.org/wp-content/uploads/2013/01/Theurbanchallenge.pdf

4 http://www.who.int/phe/health_topics/outdoorair/databases/en/

5 One consequences of this urban dynamic is going to be a massive extinction of smaller languages. The more people move to the cities, the more their vernacular languages become extraneous. Their children are not likely to go on speaking the mother tongue.

I made a study of how many of the world's supposedly 7,000 languages are actually used in today's *classrooms*. The results were eye-opening: in primary schools 400-600 languages are used. In secondary schools 200-300 are used, whereas in universities fewer than 50 languages are used. By the year 2100, these will nearly dominate the globe—especially in the cities. They are (in alphabetical order): Afrikaans, Amharic, Arabic, Bengali, Bulgarian, Burmese, Cambodian, Chinese (Mandarin), Czech, Danish, Dutch, English, Farsi, Finnish, French, German, Greek, Hebrew, Hindi, Hungarian, Indonesian, Italian, Japanese, Korean, Norwegian, Polish, Portuguese, Romanian, Russian, Serbo-Croatian, Sinhalese, Slovak, Slovenian, Spanish, Swahili, Swedish, Tamil, Thai, Turkish, Ukrainian, Urdu, Vietnamese.

6 Raymond Bakke with Jim Hart, *The Urban Christian* (MARC Europe, 1987), pp. 22-23

7 *The New Bible Commentary: Revised* (Grand Rapids, Mich.: Eerdmans, 1970), p. 91

8 *The New Bible Dictionary* (Grand Rapids, Mich.: Eerdmans, 1962), pp. 40-41

9 *The New Bible Dictionary* (Grand Rapids, Mich.: Eerdmans, 1962), p. 1240

10 Samuel Chadwick, *The Way to Pentecost* (reprint, Dixon, Mo.: Rare Christian Books, n.d.), p. 19.

11 Jim Cymbala with Dean Merrill, *Fresh Wind, Fresh Fire* (Grand Rapids, Mich.: Zondervan, 1997), p. 25.

12 Jeremy Weber, "Something Better than Revival," *Christianity Today,* June 2010, p. 38.

13 www.urbanleaders.org/weburblead2/Readings/Evangelism%20(Ghana).htm.

14 www.urbanleaders.org/weburblead2/Readings/Evangelism%20(Ghana).htm.

15 See Bessenecker's book *The New Friars* (InterVarsity, 2006) and Living Mission: the Vision and Voices of the New Friars (InterVarsity, 2010); also see *Christianity Today's* cover story "Chaos and Grace in the Slums of the Earth" by Kent Annan (September 2013, pp. 24-32).

[16] Address on "Developing a Poor People's Church" at MoveIn Conference 2014, Toronto.

[17] http://www.merriam-webster.com/dictionary/diaspora

[18] http://www.ywamsanfrancisco.org/wp-content/uploads/2013/01/Theurbanchallenge.pdf

[19] For a ranking of the world's largest congregations (by weekly attendance), see http://leadnet.org/world.

[20] *The Interlinear Literal Translation of the Greek New Testament* (Zondervan, 1952), p. 87.

[21] Bakke and Hart, p. 94.

[22] Bakke and Hart, p. 104.

[23] See "And the Walls Came Tumbling Down in China's 'Jerusalem'" by Kate Tracy, http://www.christianitytoday.com/gleanings/2014/may/walls-came-tumbling-down-china-jerusalem-wenzhou-sanjiang.html See also the New York Times report at http://www.nytimes.com/2014/05/30/world/asia/church-state-clash-in-china-coalesces-around-a-toppled-spire.html?_r=0

[24] From his "Movement Day 2013" address to a conference of more than 1,000 church leaders passionate about working for the good of their cities. The event was organized by the New York City Leadership Center.

[25] Philippines (3 cities), Thailand, Cambodia, India (5 cities), Kenya, Uganda (2 cities), Rwanda, Ghana, Bolivia, Guatemala, Dominican Republic, plus an alliance arrangement with partners in Ecuador and Peru.

[26] Per national CBS newscaster Dan Rather in a 2010 series called "Pornland."

[27] "Portland's Quiet Abolitionists" by Katelyn Beaty, *Christianity Today* (Nov. 2011), pp. 26-30.

[28] "Place of refuge to revitalise broken lives" by Graham Young, *Birmingham Mail,* June 21, 2014.

[29] Virgil Gulker with Kevin Perrotta, *Help Is Just Around the Corner* (Altamonte Springs, Fla.: Creation House, 1988), pp. 48-49.

[30] http://www.ywamsanfrancisco.org/wp-content/uploads/2013/01/Theurbanchallenge.pdf

[31] "MANI 2011 Abuja, Nigeria—A Continental Commitment to World Evangelization" by Bruce Koch, in *Mission Frontiers,* Nov. 1, 2011.

[32] Andrew Rick, "Mission from Africa," *The New York Times* (April 12, 2009).

[33] "God of This City" by Aaron Boyd, Andrew McCann, Ian Jordan, Peter Comfort, Peter Kernoghan, and Richard Bleakley. © 2006 sixsteps Music (admin. by Capitol CMG Publishing) worshiptogether.com songs (admin. by Capitol CMG Publishing).

Featured Ministries

Many ministries are serving people in cities around the world. Here is a list of some of the key ministries featured in this book:

Organization	URL	Page
Accord Network	www.accordnetwork.org	51
African Enterprise	www.africanenterprise.com	12
Apostolic Discipleship Movement	www.apostolicdiscipleshipmovement.org	67
Azusa Pacific University	www.apu.edu	54
Back to Jerusalem	www.backtojerusalem.com	91
Betel International	www.betelinternational.org	83
Bethel University	www.bethel.edu	45
Billy Graham Evangelistic Association	www.billygraham.org	45
Brooklyn Tabernacle	www.brooklyntabernacle.org	32
Church Integration Ministries (Copenhagen)	http://www.worldea.org/whoweare/leadership/hans-henrik-lund	60
City Vision	www.cityvisiontc.org	43
Compassion International	www.compassion.com	53
Convoy of Hope	www.convoyofhope.org	52
Crown College	www.crown.edu	45
Dorothea Mission	www.dorothea.org.za/	9
Ebenezer's Coffeehouse	www.ebenezerscoffeehouse.com	70
Elam Ministries	www.elam.com	71
Future of the Global Church	www.thefutureoftheglobalchurch.org	47
Gemeinsam für Berlin	www.gfberlin.de	77
GMI	www.gmi.org	ii
Hilfe Für die Brüder	www.gottes-liebe-weltweit.de	51
Hope International	www.hopeinternational.org	52
International Justice Mission	www.ijm.org	77

Organization	URL	Page
InterVarsity Christian Fellowship	www.intervarsity.org	53
Istanbul Protestant Church Foundation	www.istpcf.org	72
Kensington Temple	www.kt.org	68
Kiev Church	www.godembassy.com	71
LifeWay Research	www.lifewayresearch.com	iv
Love INC	www.loveinc.org	86
Mission India	www.missionindia.org	52
Moveln	www.movein.to/	55
National Community Church	www.theaterchurch.com	70
North Central University	www.northcentral.edu	45
Operation Mobilization	www.om.org	13
Operation World	www.operationworld.org	12
Opportunity International	www.opportunity.org	52
Oregon Center for Christian Voices	www.occv.org	78
Redeemed Christian Church of God	www.trccg.org/rccg	91
Salvation Army	www.salvationarmy.org	51
Tearfund	www.tearfund.org	51
Universities and Colleges Christian Fellowship	www.uccf.org.uk	9
University of Northwestern St. Paul	www.unwsp.edu	45
Urban Nations Outreach	www.urbanimpact.wix.com/urbannationsoutreach	59
Urban Neighbors of Hope	www.unoh.org	50
WEC International	www.wecinternational.org.uk	15
World Concern	www.worldconcern.org	51
Yoido Full Gospel Church	http://english.fgtv.com	65
Youth with a Mission	www.ywam.org	8
Zwemer Center	www.zwemercenter.com	46

Going Deeper:
Resources From GMI

The Future of the Global Church

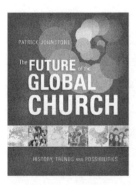

By Patrick Johnstone (book, eBook or DVD collection)

If you enjoyed the powerful insights from Patrick Johnstone in Serving God in Today's Cities (the first book in the "Engaging Challenges Facing the Global Church" series) your next step is to purchase The Future of the Global Church. Weaving together research in trends, history, demographics and religion, this thoroughly illustrated and thought-provoking resource reveals likely scenarios we may face in the next forty years as we face increasing global urbanization, water shortages, and an unprecedented number of refugees. Created by veteran researcher and missiologist Patrick Johnstone, this acclaimed resource will prepare you to face tomorrow. Johnstone brings the insights from years of publishing Operation World to the important resource.

www.gmi.org/fgc

Operation World

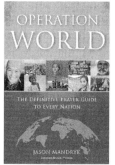

This popular and acclaimed resource—available in various formats—gathers together data on religion and people groups in every nation of the world so you can pray and prepare to reach them.

"*Operation World* has been one of the greatest tools for prayer mobilization for our world ever since it was first published." – Dr. Joseph D'souza, All India Christian Council and India Group of OM Ministries

"This longstanding and trusted resource cuts through the fog to provide an up-to-date snapshot of what in the world God is doing among the peoples. *Operation World* will become one of your most valuable books for understanding the nations and how to pray for them!" – J. D. Payne, national missionary, North American Mission Board; Associate Professor of Church Planting and Evangelism, The Southern Baptist Theological Seminary

www.gmi.org/operationworld

Where There Is Now A Church

by James Nelson, Editor

Five years ago, Christians serving in Muslim lands told their stories of challenge and change in the acclaimed *Where There Was No Church*.

Now, devoted workers provide even more detailed dispatches, stories of praise and imprisonment, and portraits of the spread of the Christian movement, including a growing church in the shadow of a mosque.

Where There Is Now A Church features questions for reflection and discussion as well as a detailed description of the best outreach practices as determined through input from hundreds of church planters surveyed by Fruitful Practice Research.

This book will encourage veteran workers and inspire new servants to reach God's children throughout the Muslim world.

http://www.gmi.org/products/books/gmibooks/where-there-now-church/

Crossing Cultures with Ruth

By James Nelson

"Your people shall be my people." When Ruth the Moabite said these powerful words, she was modeling a form of cross-cultural life that is essential for men and women who seek to serve God today.

Using insights based in Nelson's years of Fruitful Practice research into the best missionary methods, *Crossing Cultures with Ruth* encourages Kingdom workers to cross cultures boldly, commit to and identify with those you serve, and learn how to remain on the field effectively for the long haul.

www.gmi.org/crossing-cultures-with-ruth

Searching to Serve: Recruiting Kingdom Workers Online

Your website is the gateway to your ministry for hundreds of future missionaries!

Based on an extensive study of nearly four hundred future missionaries conducted in the summer of 2013, *Searching to Serve* identifies the five kinds of people who search online for overseas opportunities, revealed through their use of digital media. These five kinds of people are all interested in cross-cultural service, but they couldn't be more different in their readiness for service and the kinds of information they are seeking.

www.gmi.org/searching-to-serve

Missiographics

These eye-opening infographics tell the story of global mission through words and images, making complex issues clear so you can grasp the truth, put it into action in your ministry, and explain it to your constituents. See our library of Missiographics and sign up to receive new Missiographics free by e-mail.

http://www.gmi.org/missiographics.htm

Custom Infographics

People who have seen our Missiographics have asked us if we can create similar infographics for them. The answer is yes. GMI would love to serve you with affordable and mission-focused infographics work to engage your donors, partners or internal audiences.

http://www.gmi.org/services/missiographics/custom-infographic-creation/

GMI Research

Breakthrough! Prayerful Productive Research in Your Place of Ministry

By Stan Nussbaum (2nd Edition)

This practical training manual shows you how to combine prayer and field research for a breakthrough in your ministry. Designed for missionaries who seek to discern God's direction in their work, this on-field, on-the-job training manual is available in print and electronic versions.

Breakthrough!'s unique, practical method combines field research and prayer to help missionaries gain fresh perspective about ministry challenges they face. Insights allow workers to adjust their methods and increase the possibility of a breakthrough in their work.

The *Breakthrough!* manual helps missionaries more accurately discern God's will for their ministry, focus on a recurring problem and resolve it, and remove guesswork from long-range or annual planning projects.

Breakthrough! Coaching is a twelve-week program that allows you to engage with author and missiologist Stan Nussbaum via email or Skype. (Coaching may be done as independent study or as part of an academic program such as the MA in Organizational Leadership offered by Development Associates International in partnership with selected universities.)

Breakthrough! Seminars explore research and discernment through a five-day seminar featuring half-day group sessions. Participants will design research projects they will conduct on their own for three to six months. The group learning atmosphere in a seminar is helpful to many first-time researchers.

http://www.gmi.org/products/books/breakthrough/

Global Briefing: A Fresh Look at God's World

Christians are called to "Go into all the world." But which world? If our knowledge and research are based on outmoded information, we risk preparing ourselves to reach a world that no longer exists.

Global Briefing gives missions leaders and organizations up-to-date information on current global trends in population, migration, religion and communications technology.

Using dozens of charts, graphs and maps, *Global Briefing* illustrates today's trends in ways you can see and understand, including food production, income, freedom, distribution of charismatics and other Christian groups.

It's a big, complicated world. If you want to understand it better, contact GMI for more information on having a GMI speaker present the Global Briefing to your church, staff, leadership team or board.

http://www.gmi.org/products/research-reports/global-briefing.

To learn more about these and other resources, visit gmi.org.